4th (KING'S OWN) REGIMENT
LIGHT COMPANY
1775

Red	Coats, waistcoats
Blue	Facings, cuffs, collars
White	Button hole bindings, turnbacks, cross-belts, haversacks, breeches, stockings, hat lace, fusil slings, knapsacks
Brown	Knapsack straps, fusils
Black	Gaiters, shoes, bayonet and sword scabbards
Gray	Blanket rolls
Silver	Lieutenant's epaulette

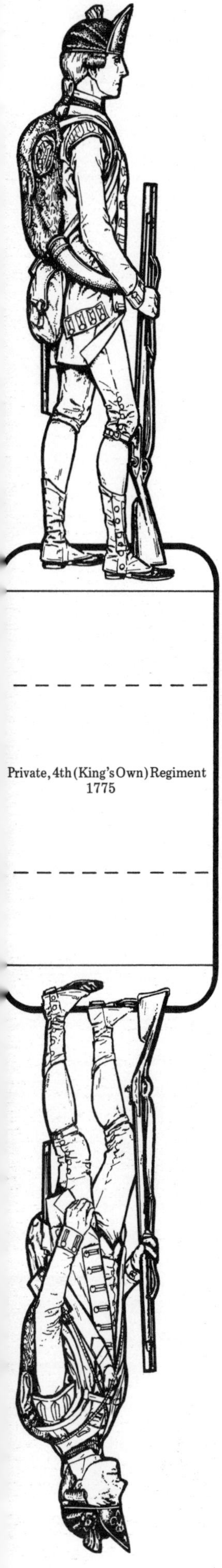
Private, 4th (King's Own) Regiment
1775

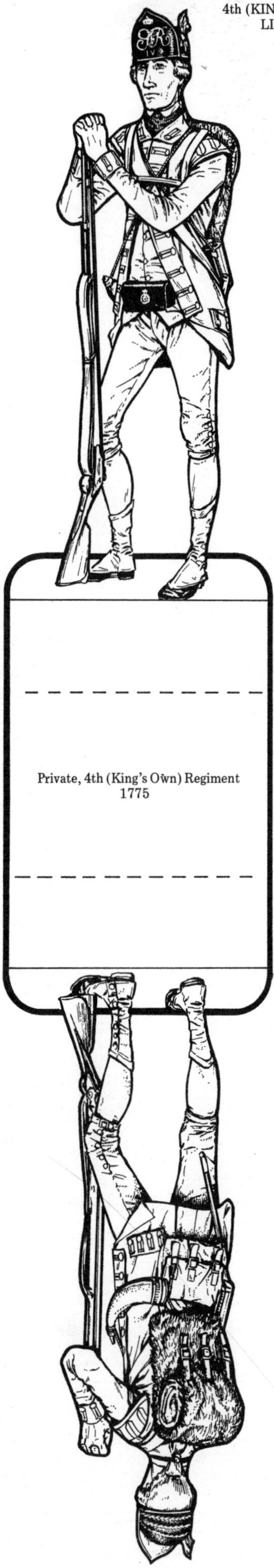
Private, 4th (King's Own) Regiment
1775

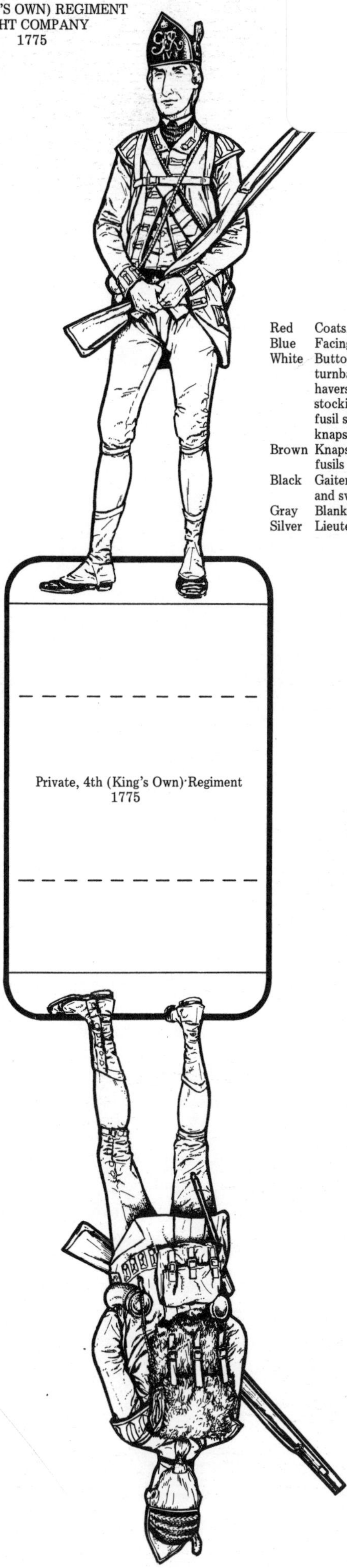
Private, 4th (King's Own) Regiment
1775

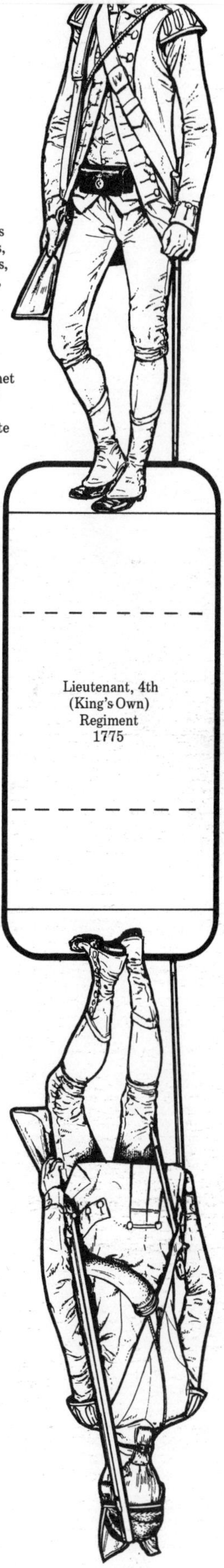
Lieutenant, 4th
(King's Own)
Regiment
1775

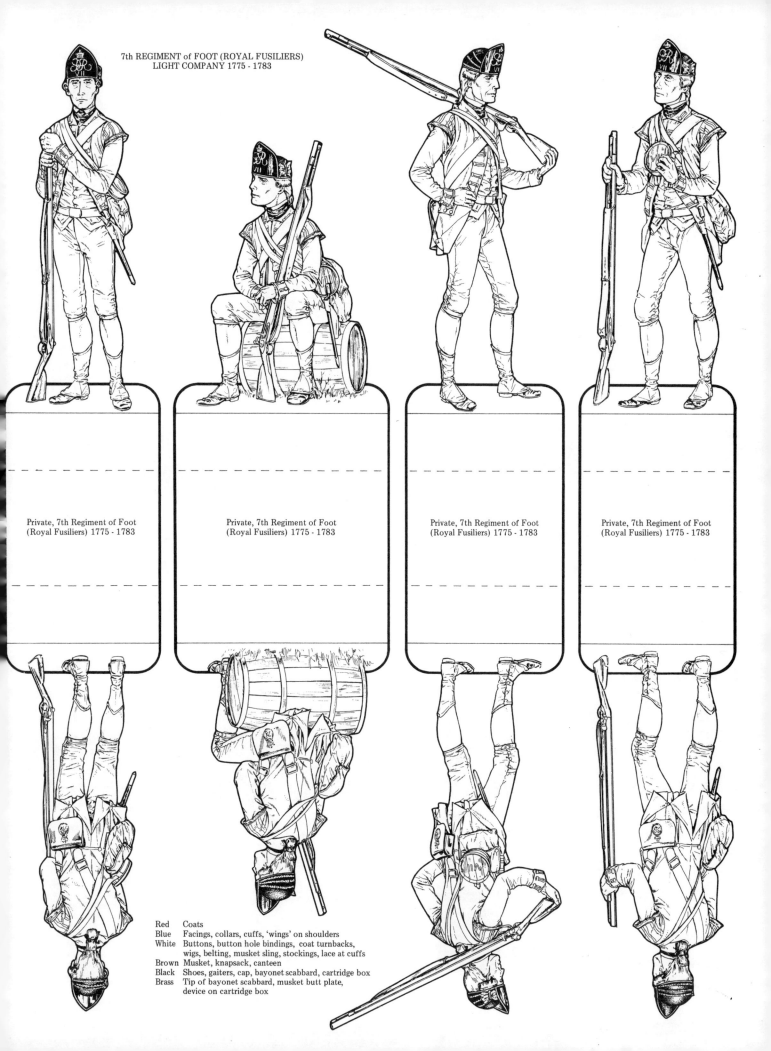

7th REGIMENT of FOOT (ROYAL FUSILIERS)
LIGHT COMPANY 1775 - 1783

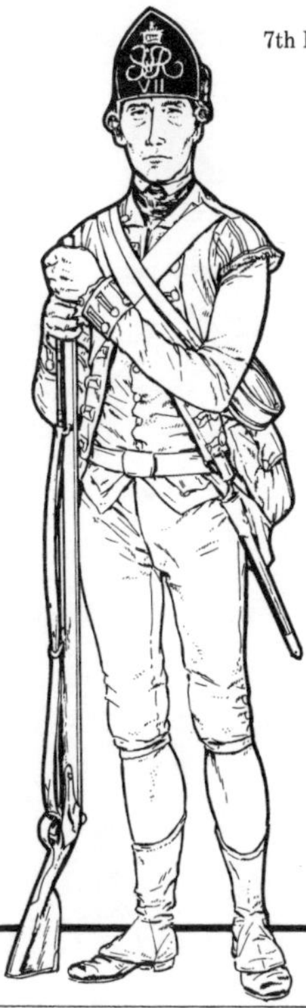
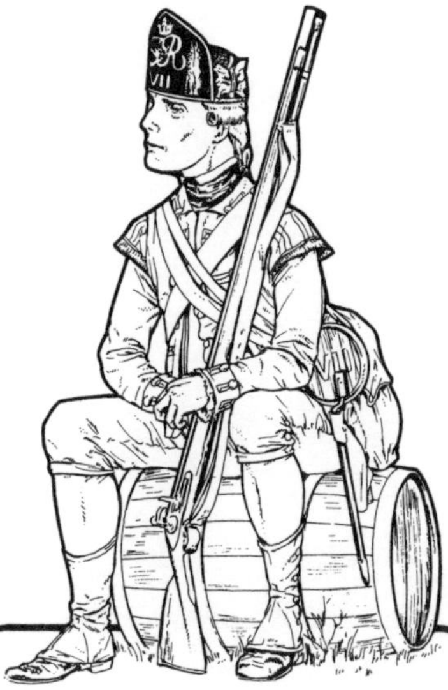
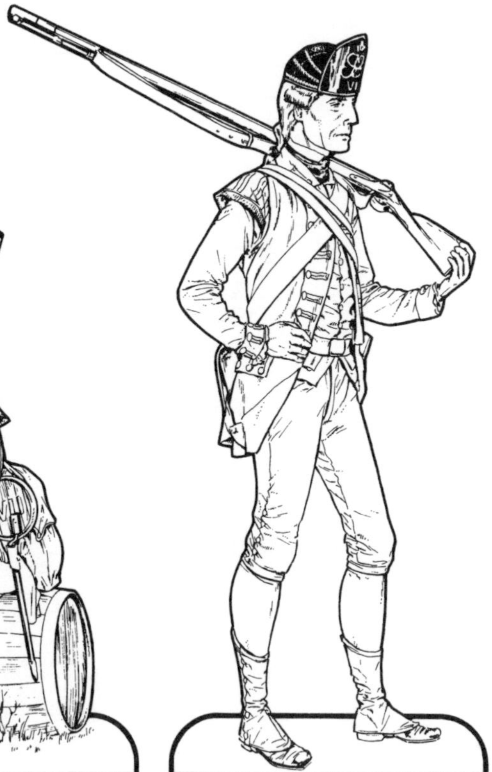
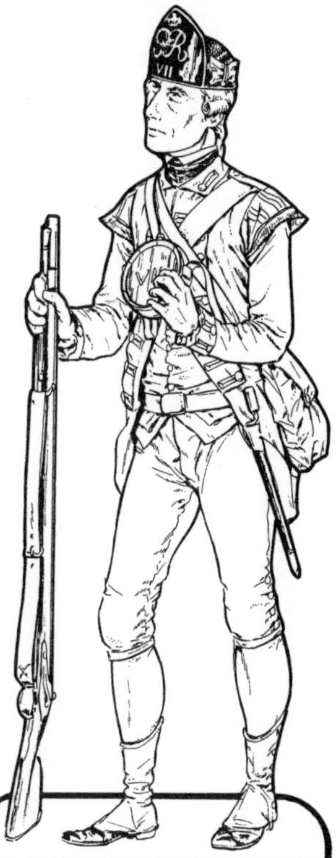

Private, 7th Regiment of Foot (Royal Fusiliers) 1775 - 1783

Private, 7th Regiment of Foot (Royal Fusiliers) 1775 - 1783

Private, 7th Regiment of Foot (Royal Fusiliers) 1775 - 1783

Private, 7th Regiment of Foot (Royal Fusiliers) 1775 - 1783

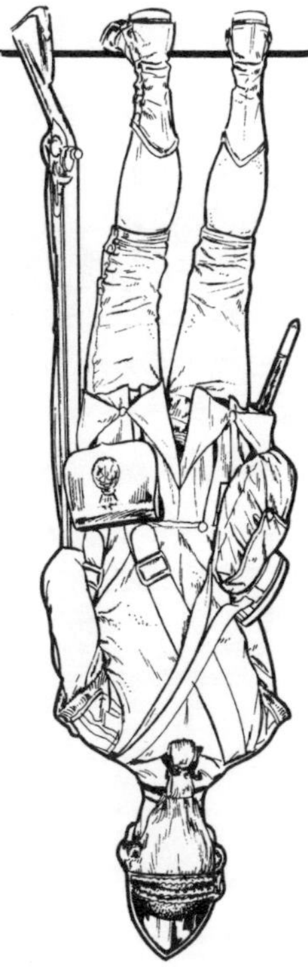
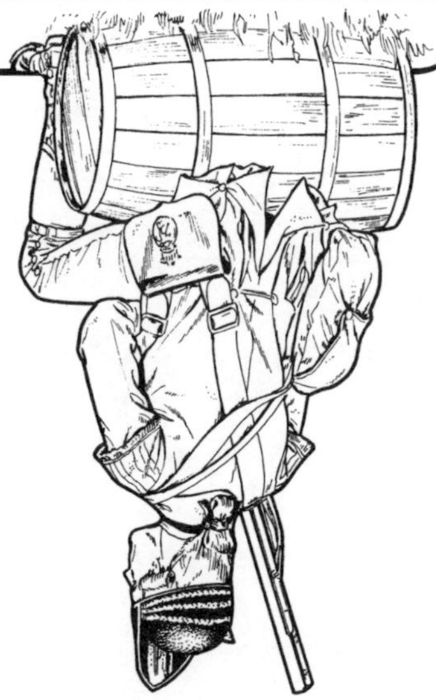
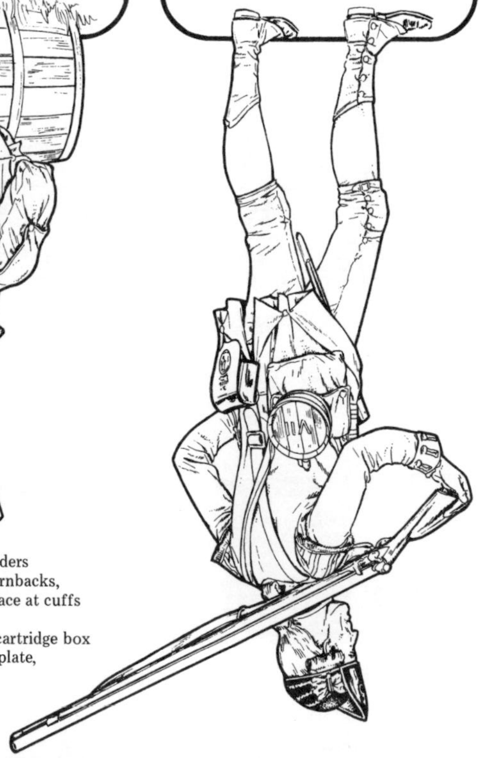
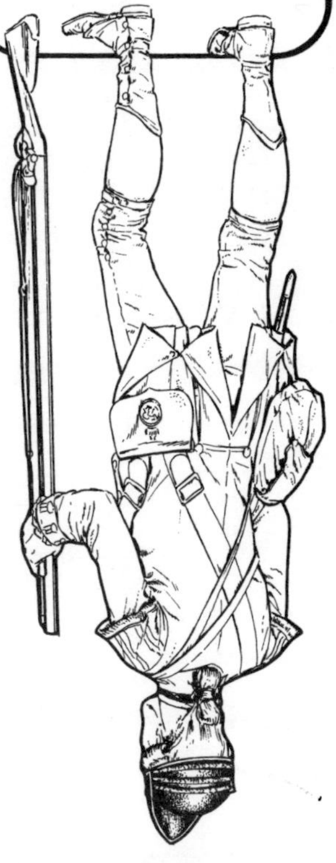

Red	Coats
Blue	Facings, collars, cuffs, 'wings' on shoulders
White	Buttons, button hole bindings, coat turnbacks, wigs, belting, musket sling, stockings, lace at cuffs
Brown	Musket, knapsack, canteen
Black	Shoes, gaiters, cap, bayonet scabbard, cartridge box
Brass	Tip of bayonet scabbard, musket butt plate, device on cartridge box

BRITISH COMMAND STAFF

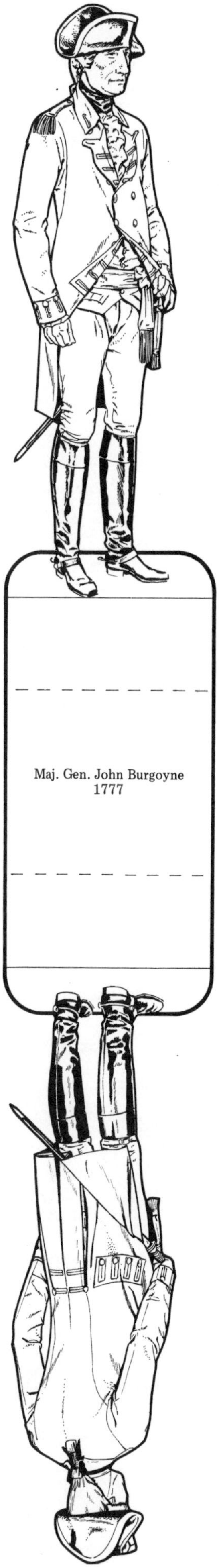
Maj. Gen. John Burgoyne
1777

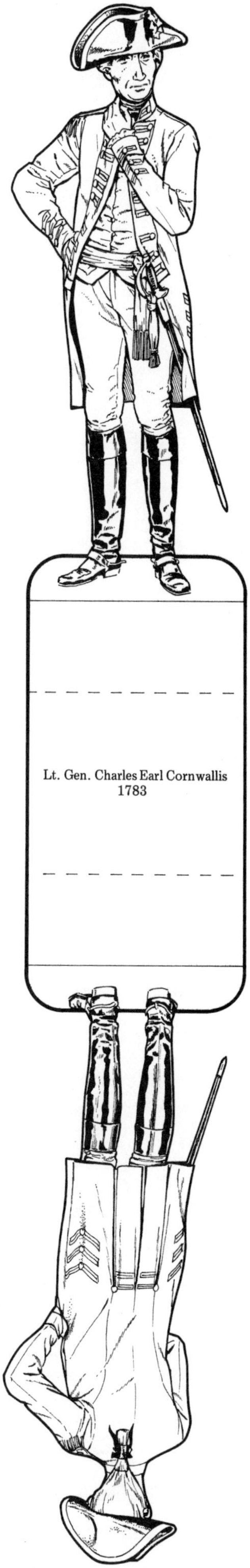
Lt. Gen. Charles Earl Cornwallis
1783

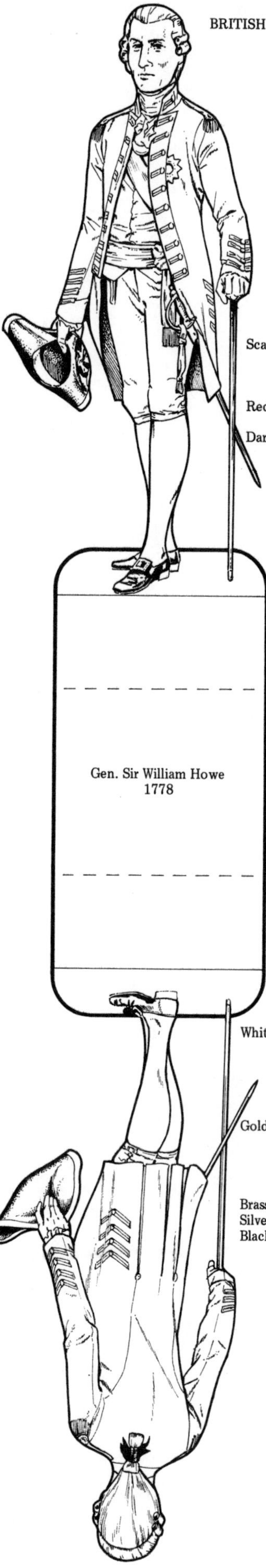
Gen. Sir William Howe
1778

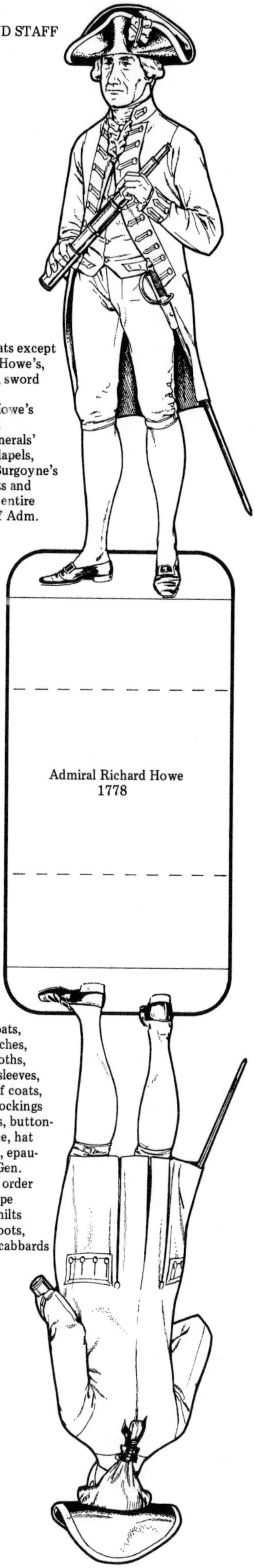
Admiral Richard Howe
1778

Scarlet	All coats except Adm. Howe's, sashes, sword knots
Red	Gen. Howe's ribbon
Dark blue	Generals' cuffs, lapels, Gen. Burgoyne's pockets and collar, entire coat of Adm. Howe
White	Waistcoats, all breeches, neck cloths, lace at sleeves, lining of coats, wigs, stockings
Gold	Buttons, button-hole lace, hat binding, epaulettes, Gen. Howe's order
Brass	Telescope
Silver	Sword hilts
Black	Hats, boots, sword scabbards

1st REGIMENT of FOOT GUARDS 1776 - 1783

Red	Coats
Blue	Coat facings, cuffs, collars
White	Lace on facings, cuffs, pockets, trim on hats, turnbacks of coats, breeches, stockings, vests, belting, musket slings, wigs
Black	Hats, gaiters, shoes, cartridge boxes, bayonet scabbards
Silver	Musket barrels
Brass	Buttons, forecap and butt plates of muskets, devices on cartridge boxes

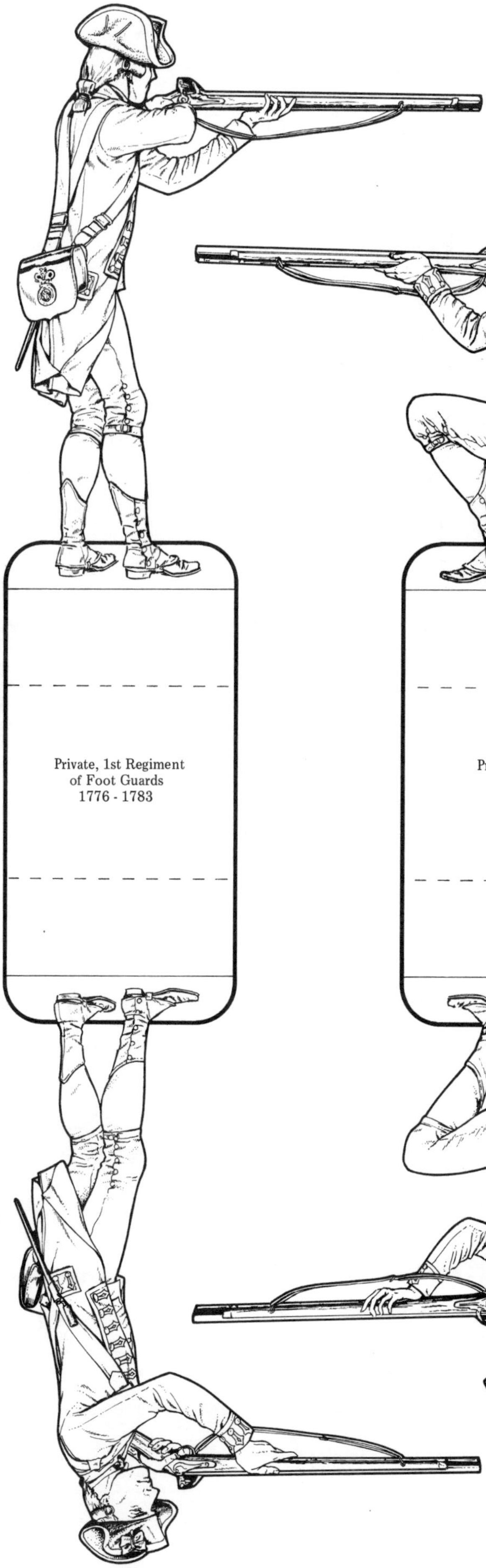
Private, 1st Regiment
of Foot Guards
1776 - 1783

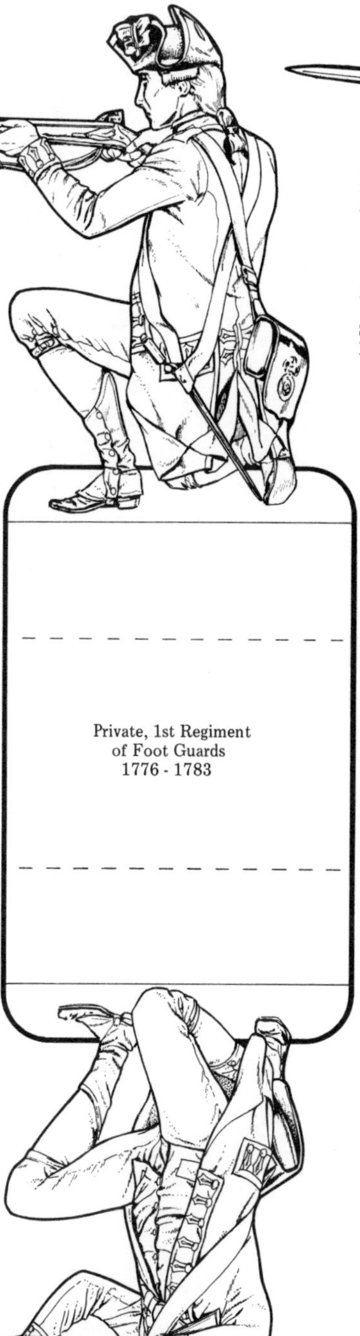
Private, 1st Regiment
of Foot Guards
1776 - 1783

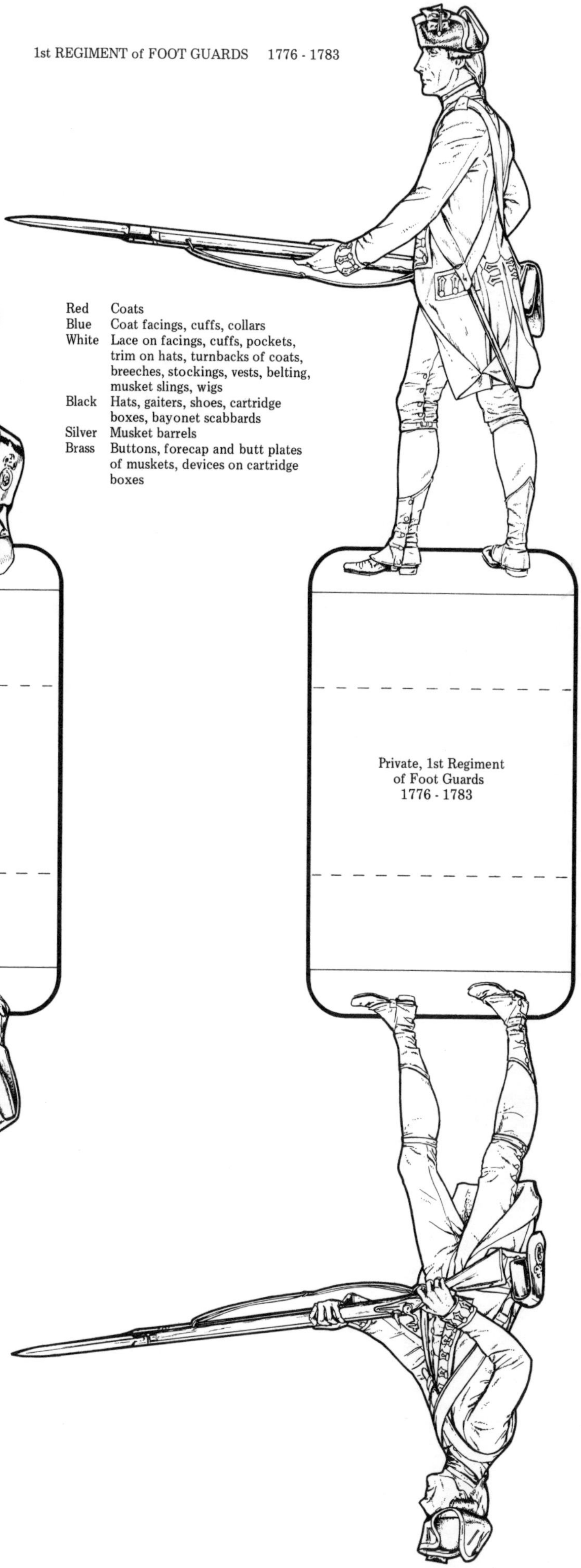
Private, 1st Regiment
of Foot Guards
1776 - 1783

17th REGIMENT of LIGHT DRAGOONS
on detached duty with Tarleton's Legion in the South, 1778.

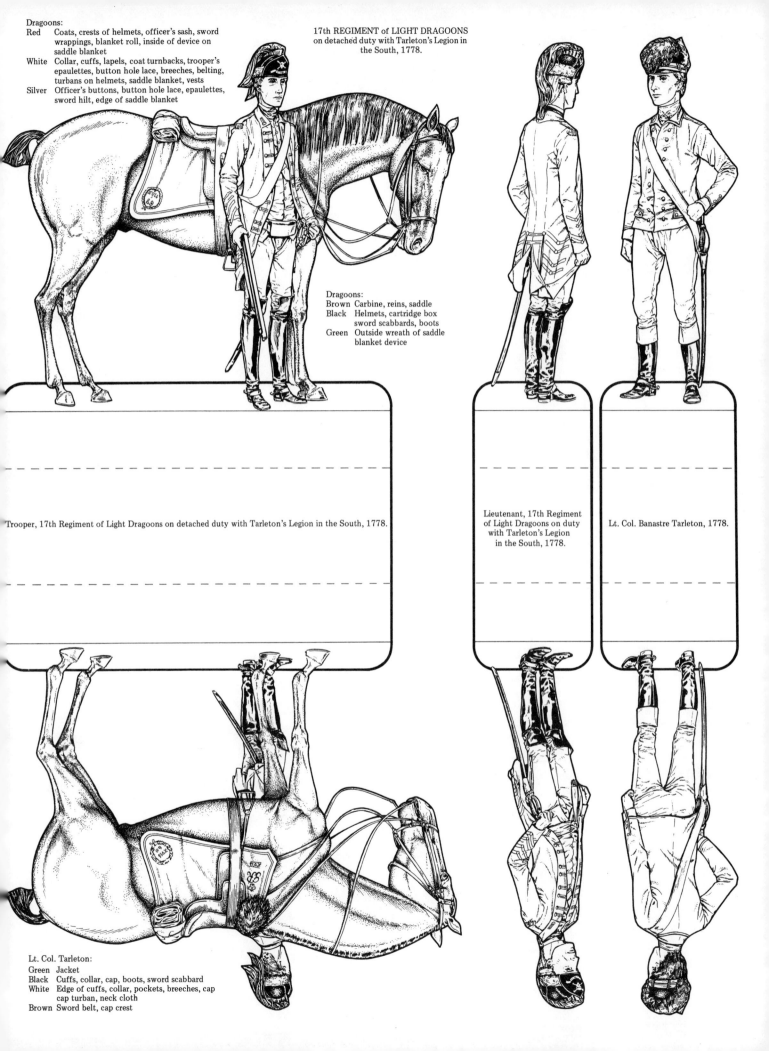

Dragoons:
Red Coats, crests of helmets, officer's sash, sword wrappings, blanket roll, inside of device on saddle blanket
White Collar, cuffs, lapels, coat turnbacks, trooper's epaulettes, button hole lace, breeches, belting, turbans on helmets, saddle blanket, vests
Silver Officer's buttons, button hole lace, epaulettes, sword hilt, edge of saddle blanket

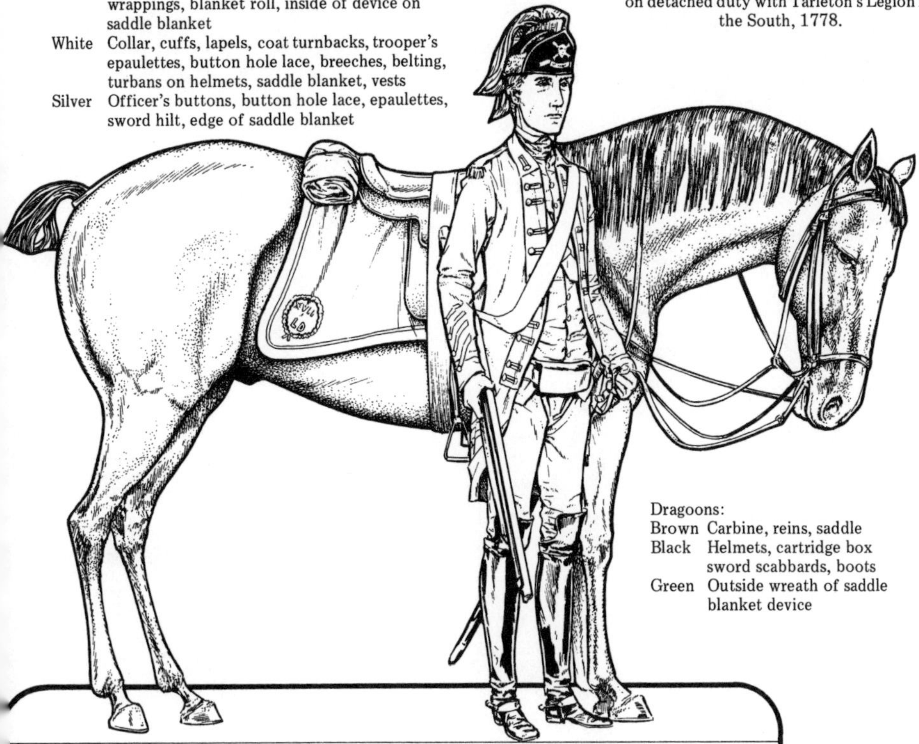

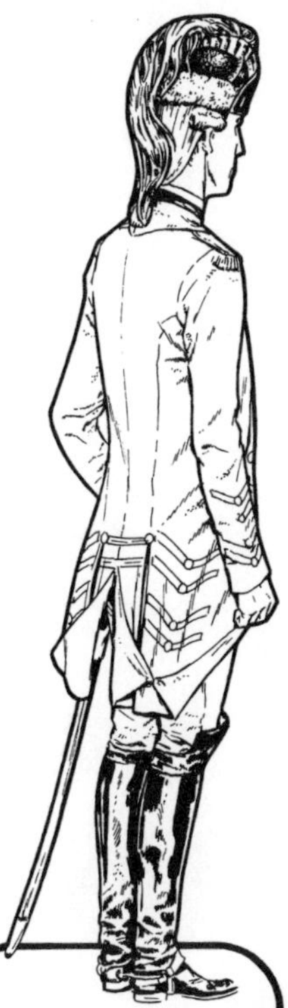

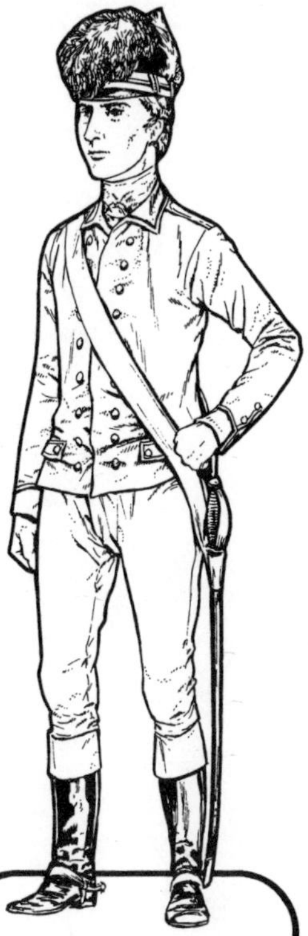

Dragoons:
Brown Carbine, reins, saddle
Black Helmets, cartridge box sword scabbards, boots
Green Outside wreath of saddle blanket device

Trooper, 17th Regiment of Light Dragoons on detached duty with Tarleton's Legion in the South, 1778.

Lieutenant, 17th Regiment of Light Dragoons on duty with Tarleton's Legion in the South, 1778.

Lt. Col. Banastre Tarleton, 1778.

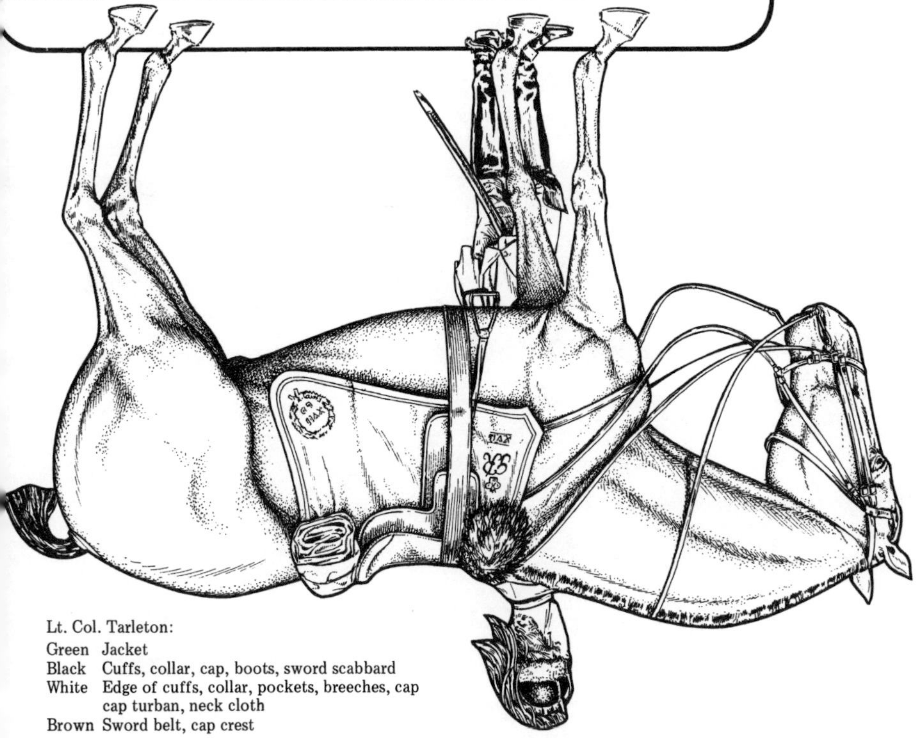

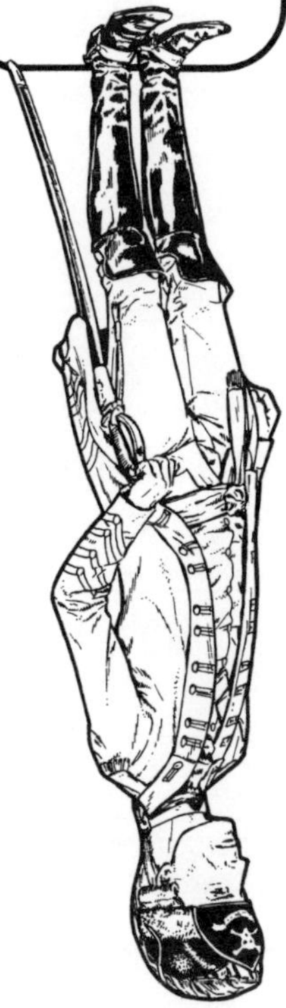

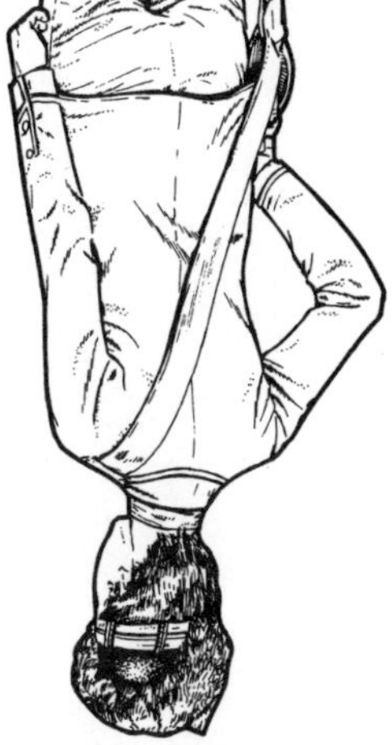

Lt. Col. Tarleton:
Green Jacket
Black Cuffs, collar, cap, boots, sword scabbard
White Edge of cuffs, collar, pockets, breeches, cap cap turban, neck cloth
Brown Sword belt, cap crest

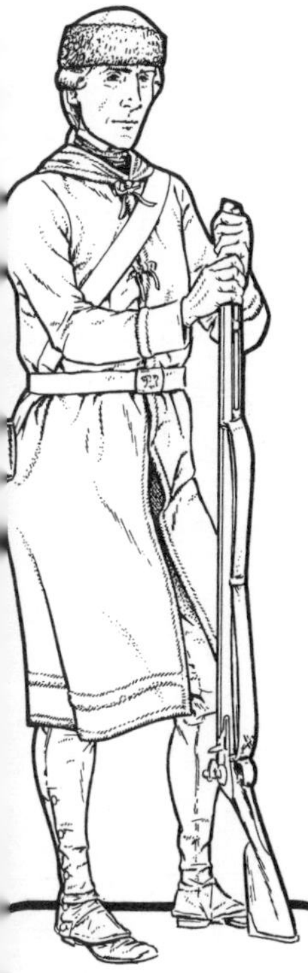

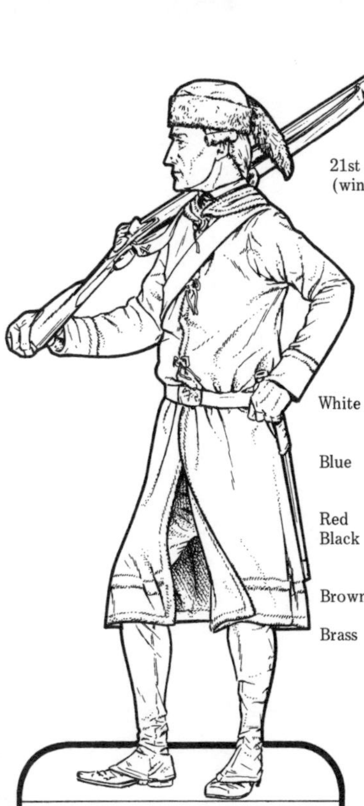

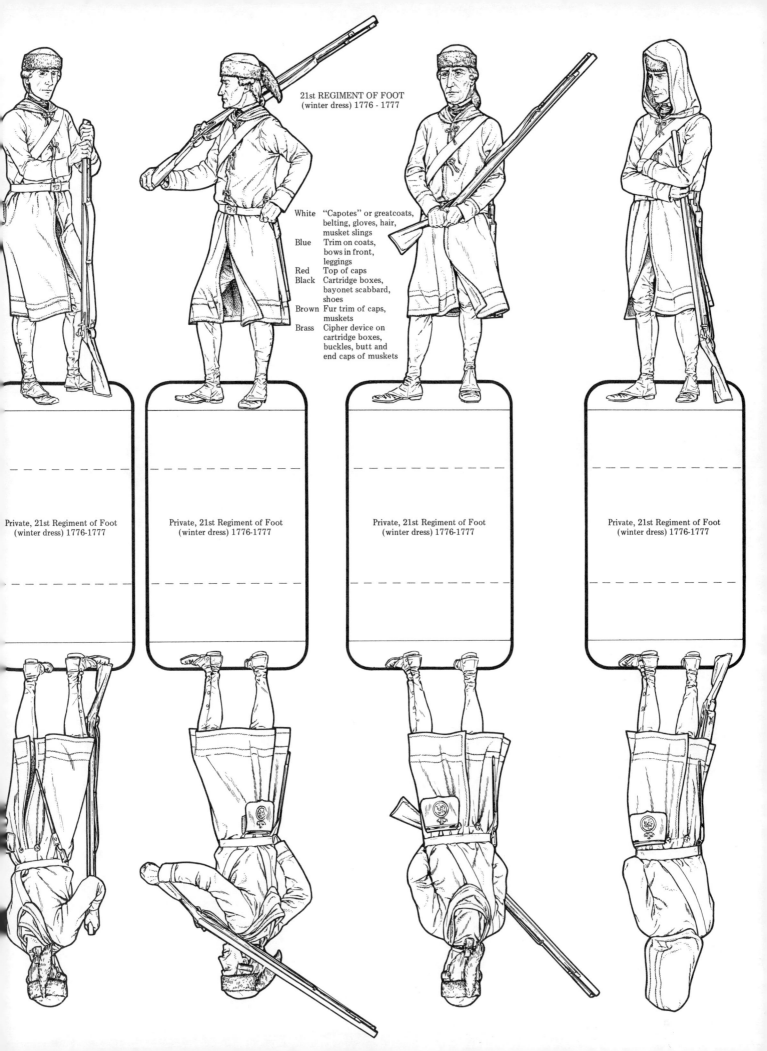

21st REGIMENT OF FOOT
(winter dress) 1776 - 1777

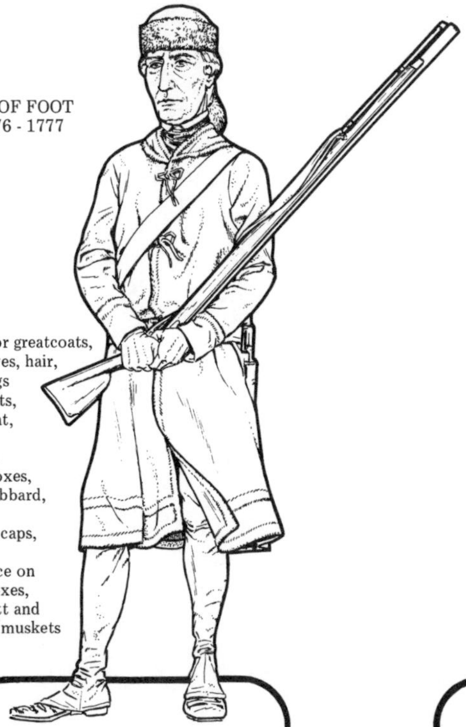

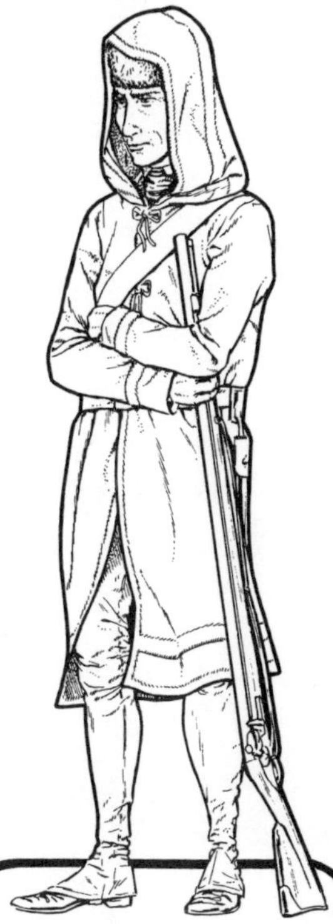

White	"Capotes" or greatcoats, belting, gloves, hair, musket slings
Blue	Trim on coats, bows in front, leggings
Red	Top of caps
Black	Cartridge boxes, bayonet scabbard, shoes
Brown	Fur trim of caps, muskets
Brass	Cipher device on cartridge boxes, buckles, butt and end caps of muskets

Private, 21st Regiment of Foot
(winter dress) 1776-1777

Private, 21st Regiment of Foot
(winter dress) 1776-1777

Private, 21st Regiment of Foot
(winter dress) 1776-1777

Private, 21st Regiment of Foot
(winter dress) 1776-1777

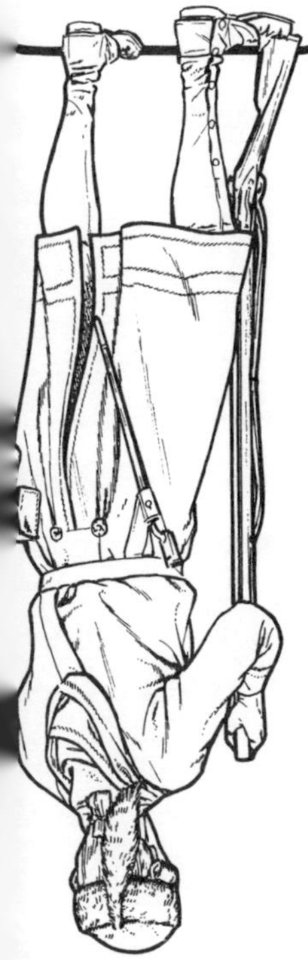

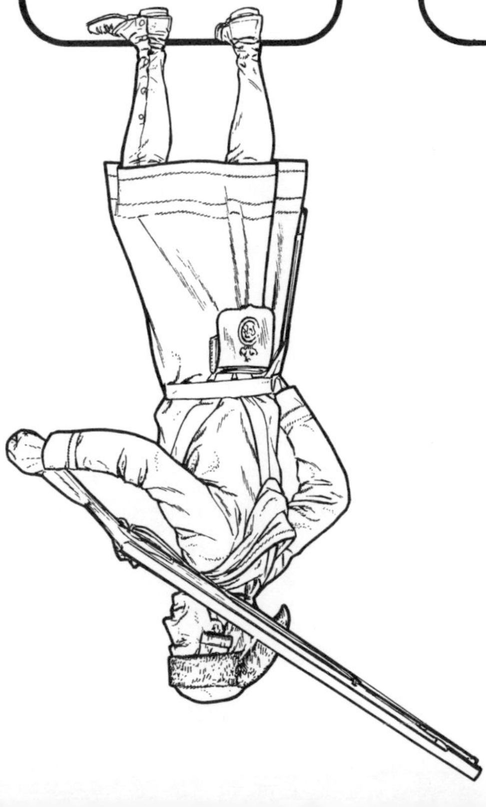

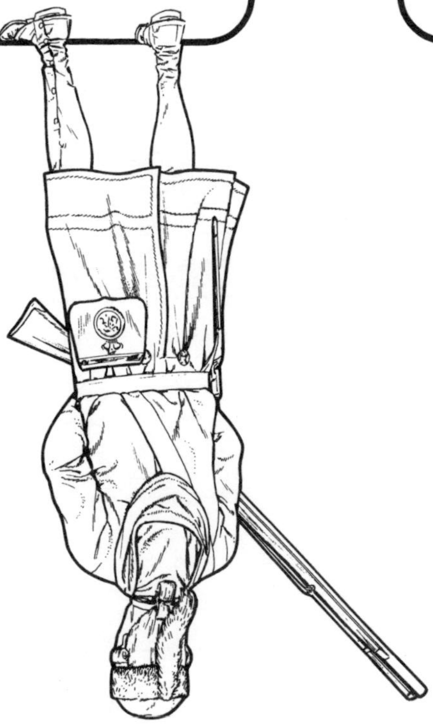

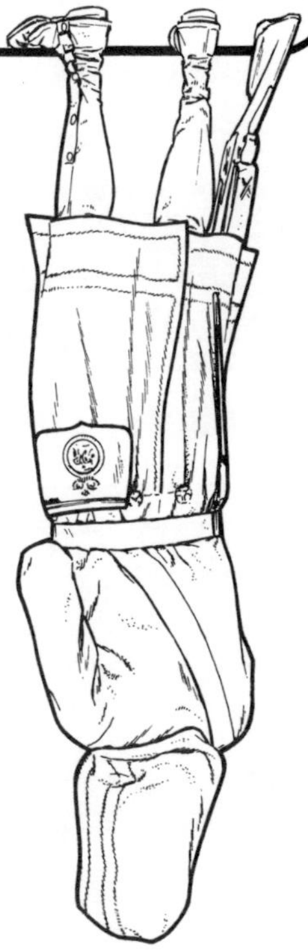

10th REGIMENT of FOOT
1775

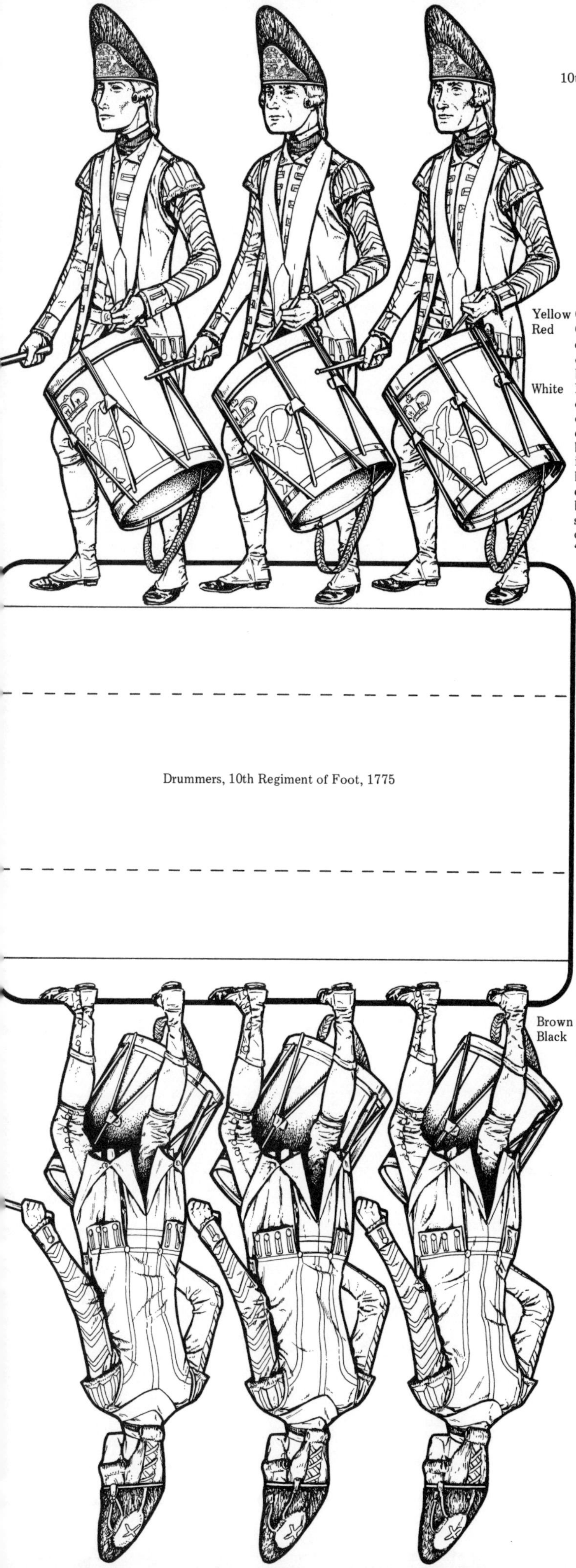
Drummers, 10th Regiment of Foot, 1775

Yellow Coats, drum fronts, fife cases
Red Coat facings, cuffs, collars, epaulettes, shoulder straps, ovals at back of caps, bands on drums
White Buttons, buttonholes, stripes on sleeves, fringe & stripes on epaulettes, lace on cuffs, waist coats, breeches, stockings, fife & drum belts, tassels on caps, wigs, turnbacks of coats, stripes on backs of coats, numeral "X" on caps

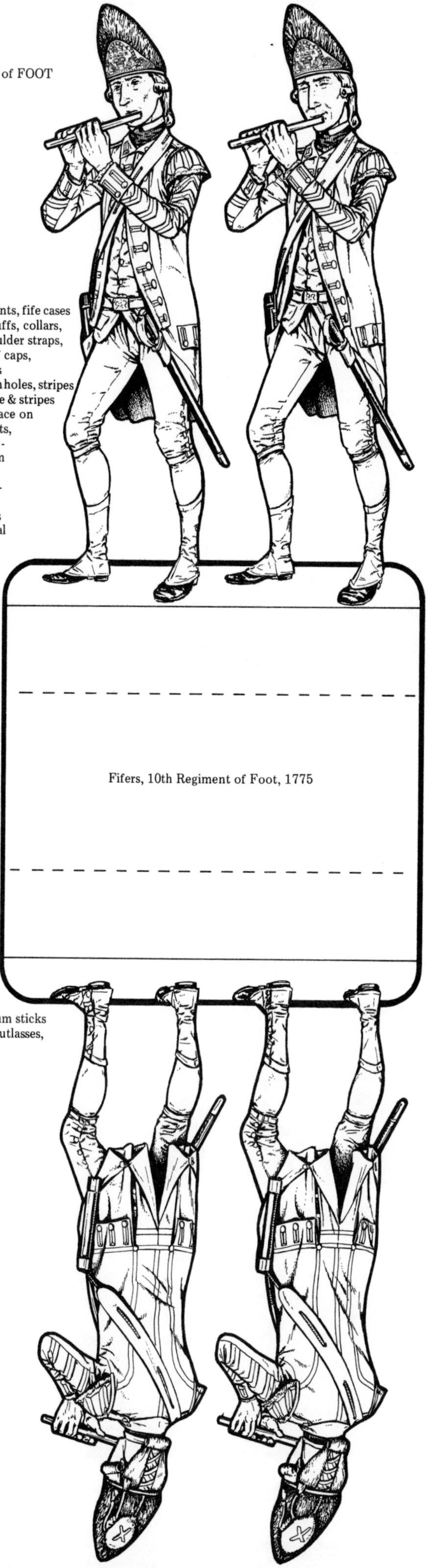
Fifers, 10th Regiment of Foot, 1775

Brown Caps, fifes, drum sticks
Black Scabbards of cutlasses, gaiters, shoes

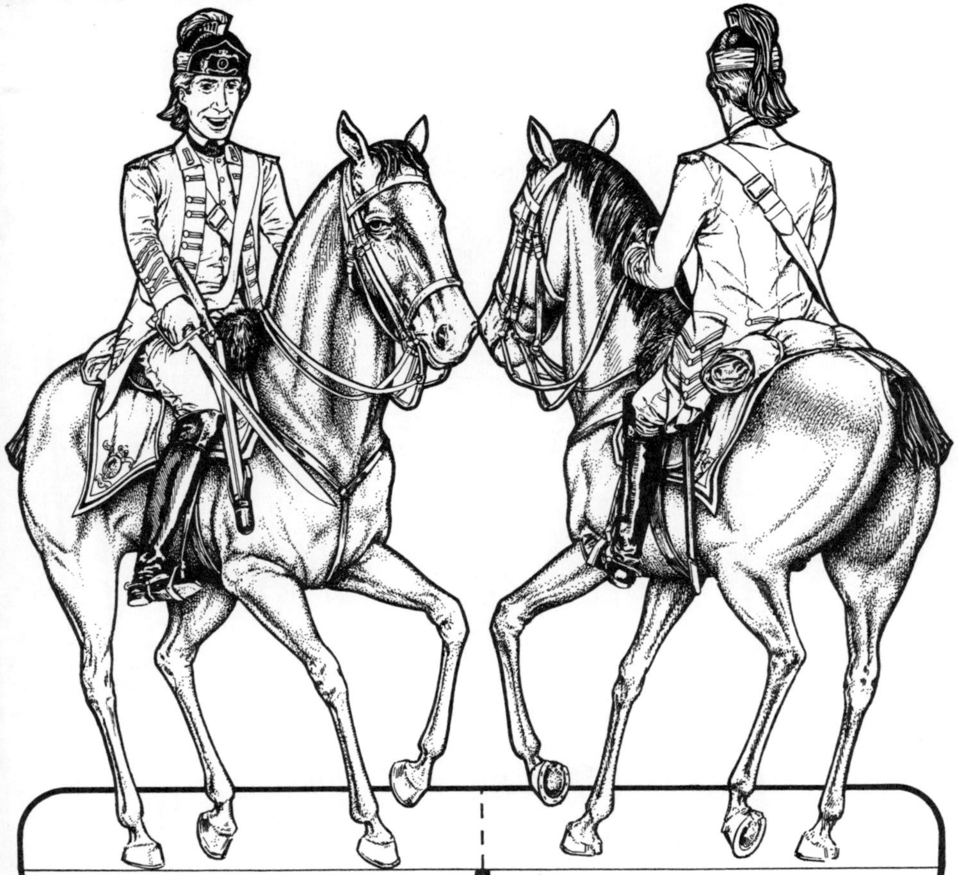

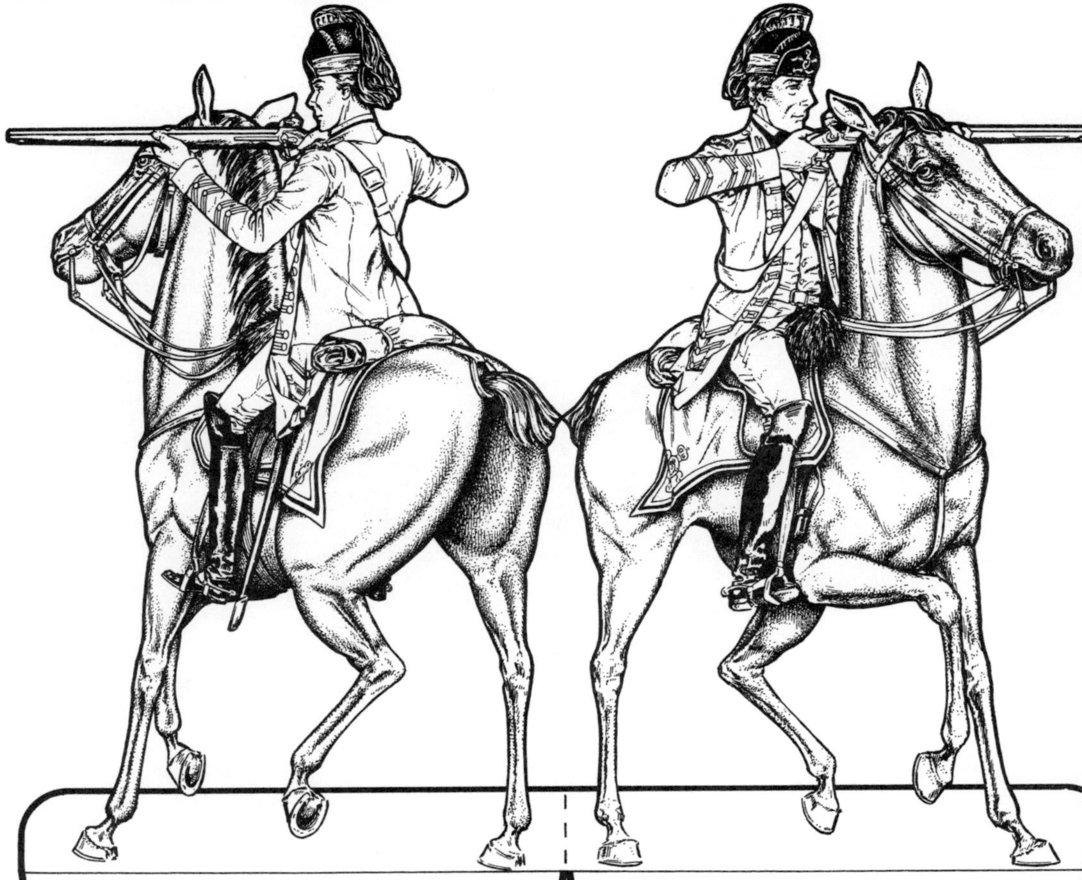

Private, 16th Light Dragoons
The Queen's, 1775 - 1783

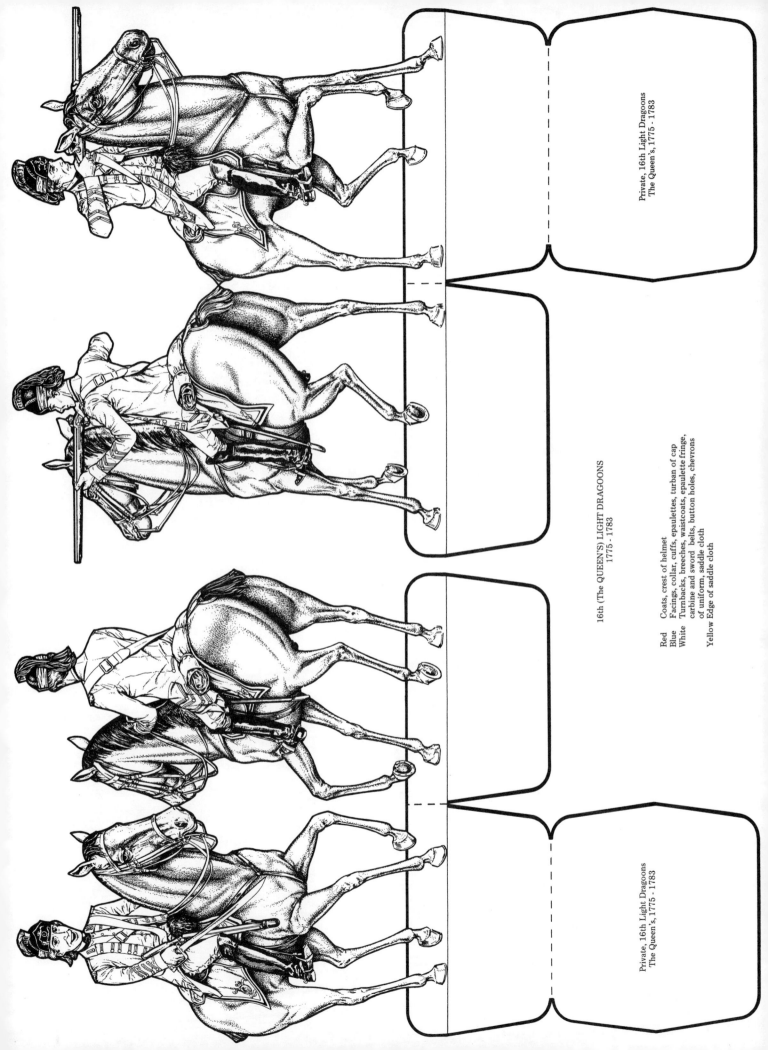

16th (The QUEEN'S) LIGHT DRAGOONS
1775 - 1783

Red	Coats, crest of helmet
Blue	Facings, collar, cuffs, epaulettes, turban of cap
White	Turnbacks, breeches, waistcoats, epaulette fringe, carbine and sword belts, button holes, chevrons of uniform, saddle cloth
Yellow	Edge of saddle cloth

Private, 16th Light Dragoons
The Queen's, 1775 - 1783

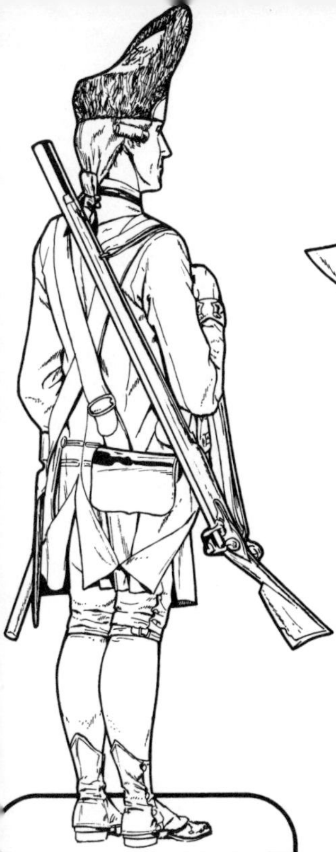

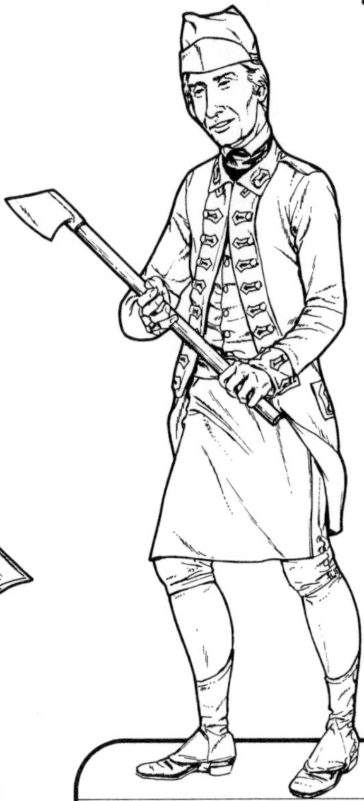

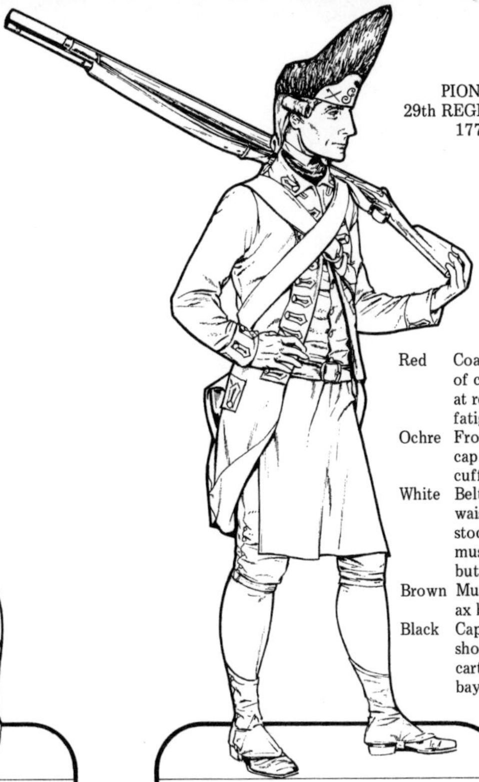

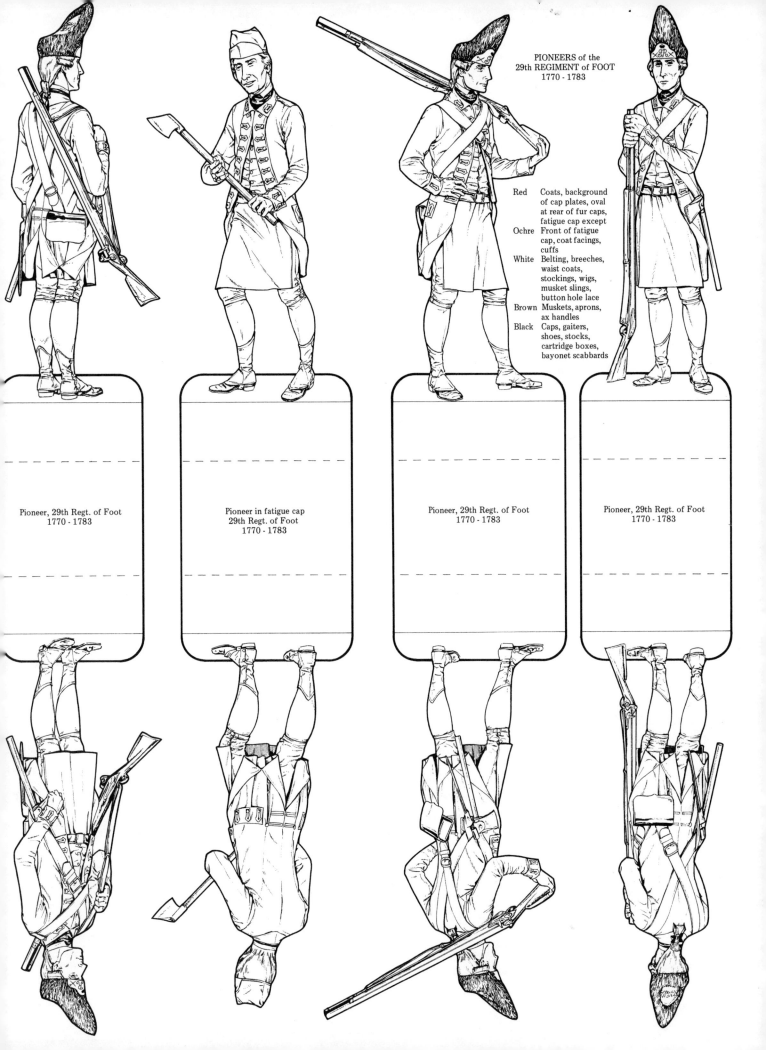

PIONEERS of the
29th REGIMENT of FOOT
1770 - 1783

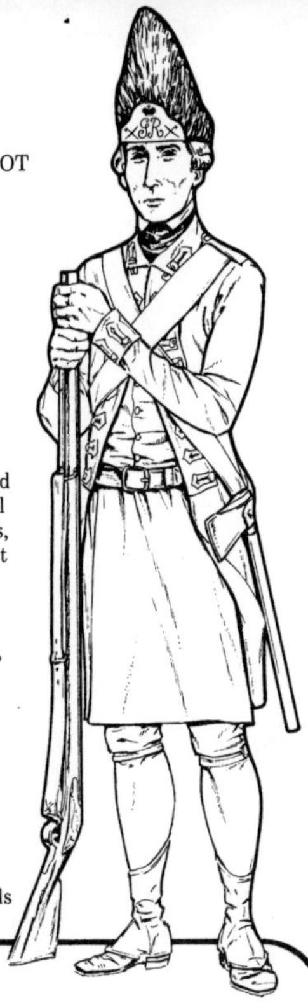

Red	Coats, background of cap plates, oval at rear of fur caps, fatigue cap except
Ochre	Front of fatigue cap, coat facings, cuffs
White	Belting, breeches, waist coats, stockings, wigs, musket slings, button hole lace
Brown	Muskets, aprons, ax handles
Black	Caps, gaiters, shoes, stocks, cartridge boxes, bayonet scabbards

Pioneer, 29th Regt. of Foot
1770 - 1783

Pioneer in fatigue cap
29th Regt. of Foot
1770 - 1783

Pioneer, 29th Regt. of Foot
1770 - 1783

Pioneer, 29th Regt. of Foot
1770 - 1783

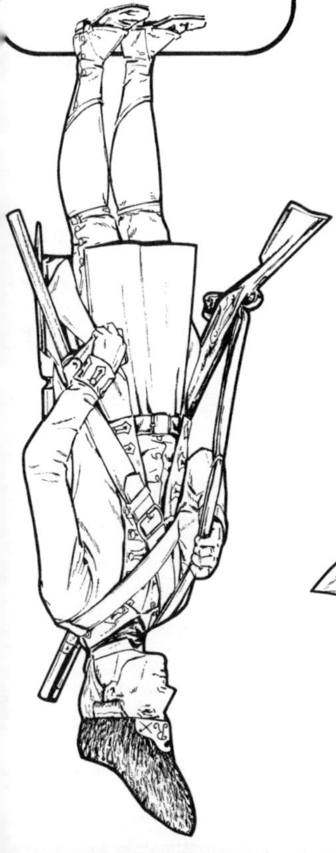

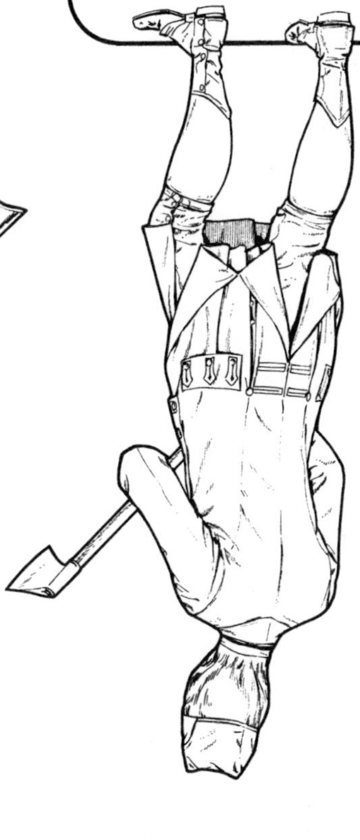

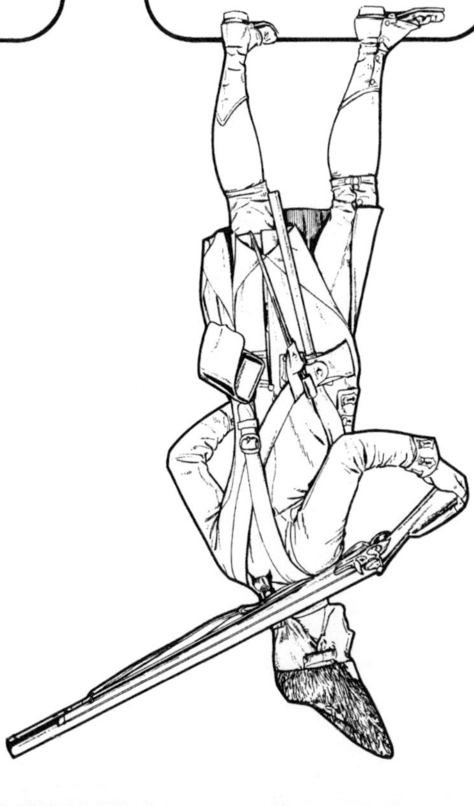

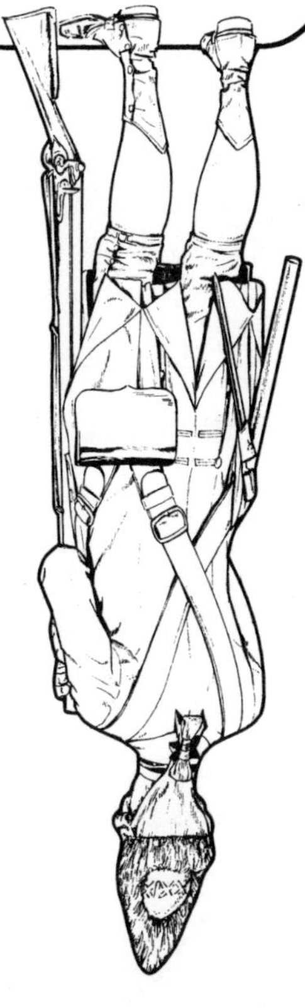

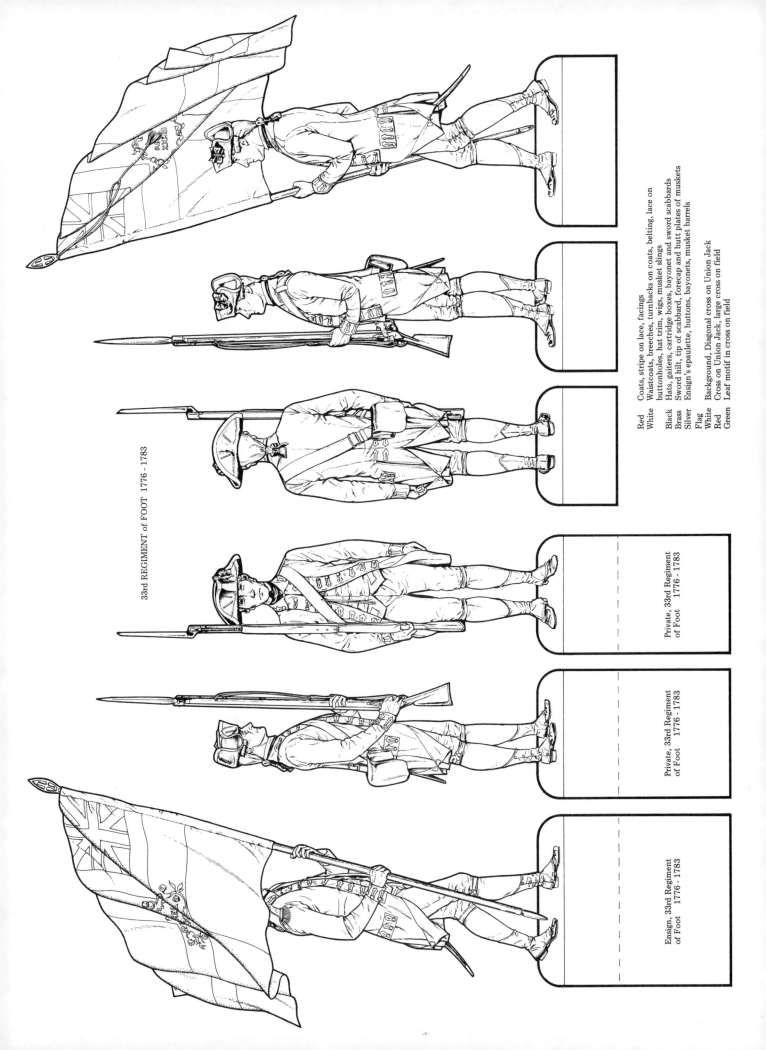

33rd REGIMENT of FOOT 1776 - 1783

Red   Coats, stripe on lace, facings
White   Waistcoats, breeches, turnbacks on coats, belting, lace on buttonholes, hat trim, wigs, musket slings
Black   Hats, gaiters, cartridge boxes, bayonet and sword scabbards
Brass   Sword hilt, tip of scabbard, forecap and butt plates of muskets
Silver   Ensign's epaulette, buttons, bayonets, musket barrels
Flag
White   Background, Diagonal cross on Union Jack
Red   Cross on Union Jack, large cross on field
Green   Leaf motif in cross on field

Private, 33rd Regiment of Foot 1776 - 1783

Private, 33rd Regiment of Foot 1776 - 1783

Ensign, 33rd Regiment of Foot 1776 - 1783

22nd REGIMENT of FOOT (MANCHESTER VOLUNTEERS) 1775 - 1783

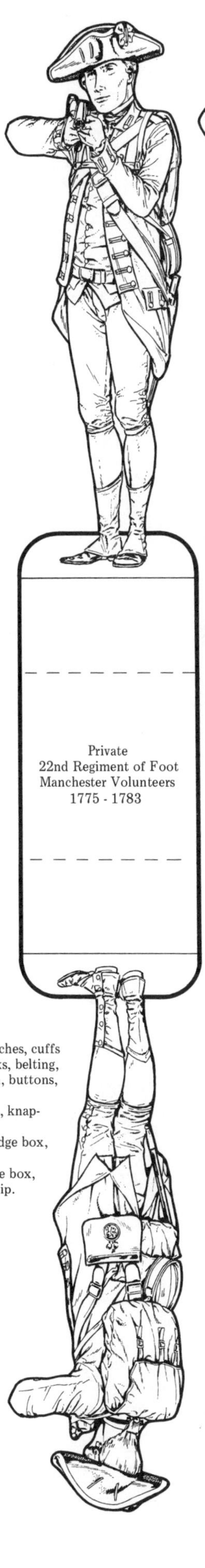
Private
22nd Regiment of Foot
Manchester Volunteers
1775 - 1783

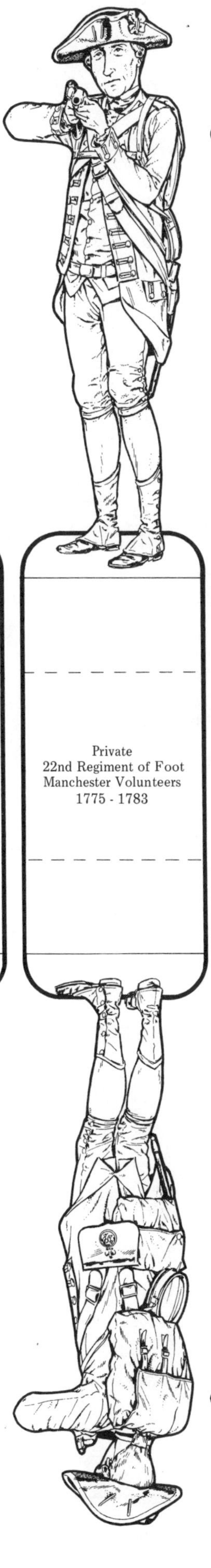
Private
22nd Regiment of Foot
Manchester Volunteers
1775 - 1783

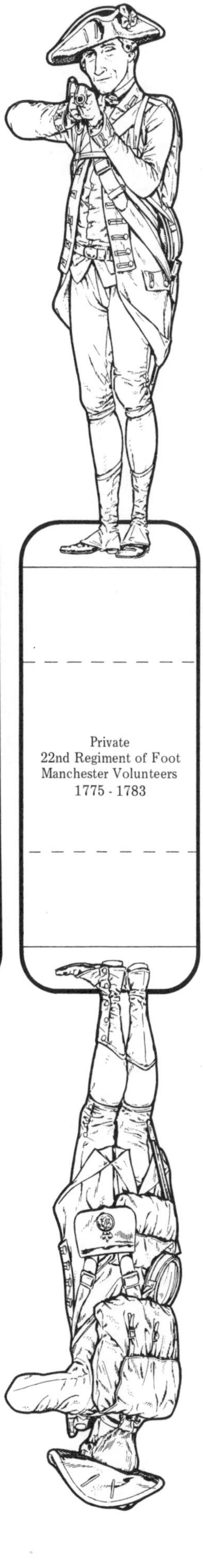
Private
22nd Regiment of Foot
Manchester Volunteers
1775 - 1783

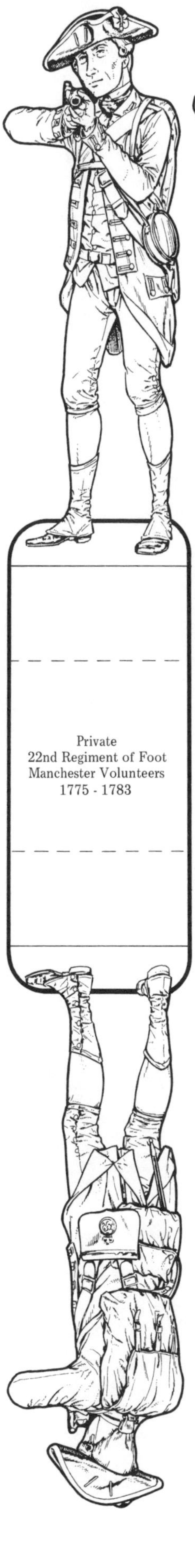
Private
22nd Regiment of Foot
Manchester Volunteers
1775 - 1783

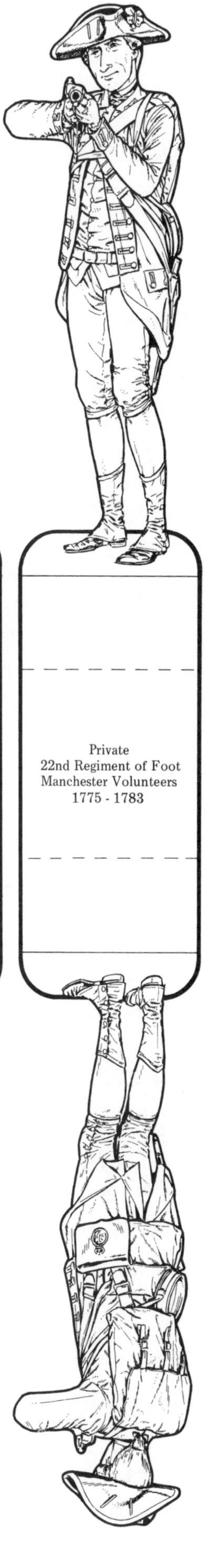
Private
22nd Regiment of Foot
Manchester Volunteers
1775 - 1783

Red	Coats
Buff	Facings, vest, breeches, cuffs
White	Coat tail, turnbacks, belting, stockings, hat trim, buttons, button holes
Brown	Canteens, muskets, knap-sack, haversack
Black	Hat, gaiters, cartridge box, bayonet scabbard
Brass	Device on cartridge box, buckles, bayonet tip.

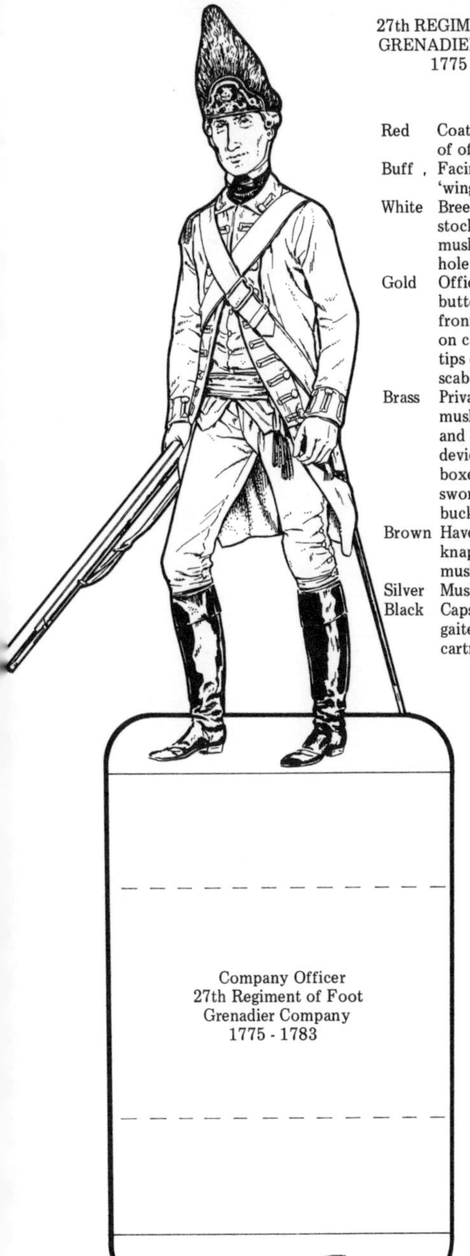

27th REGIMENT of FOOT
GRENADIER COMPANY
1775 - 1783

Red	Coats, oval at back of officer's cap, sash
Buff ,	Facings, cuffs, collars, 'wings' of privates
White	Breeches, waistcoats, stockings, wigs, belting, musket slings, button hole lace, canteens
Gold	Officer's epaulette, buttons, plate in front of caps, device on cartridge boxes, tips of sword scabbards, buckles
Brass	Privates' buttons, musket buttcaps and fore-arm caps, device on cartridge boxes, tips of sword scabbards, buckles
Brown	Haversacks, knapsacks, muskets
Silver	Musket metal
Black	Caps, shoes, boots, gaiters, scabbards, cartridge boxes

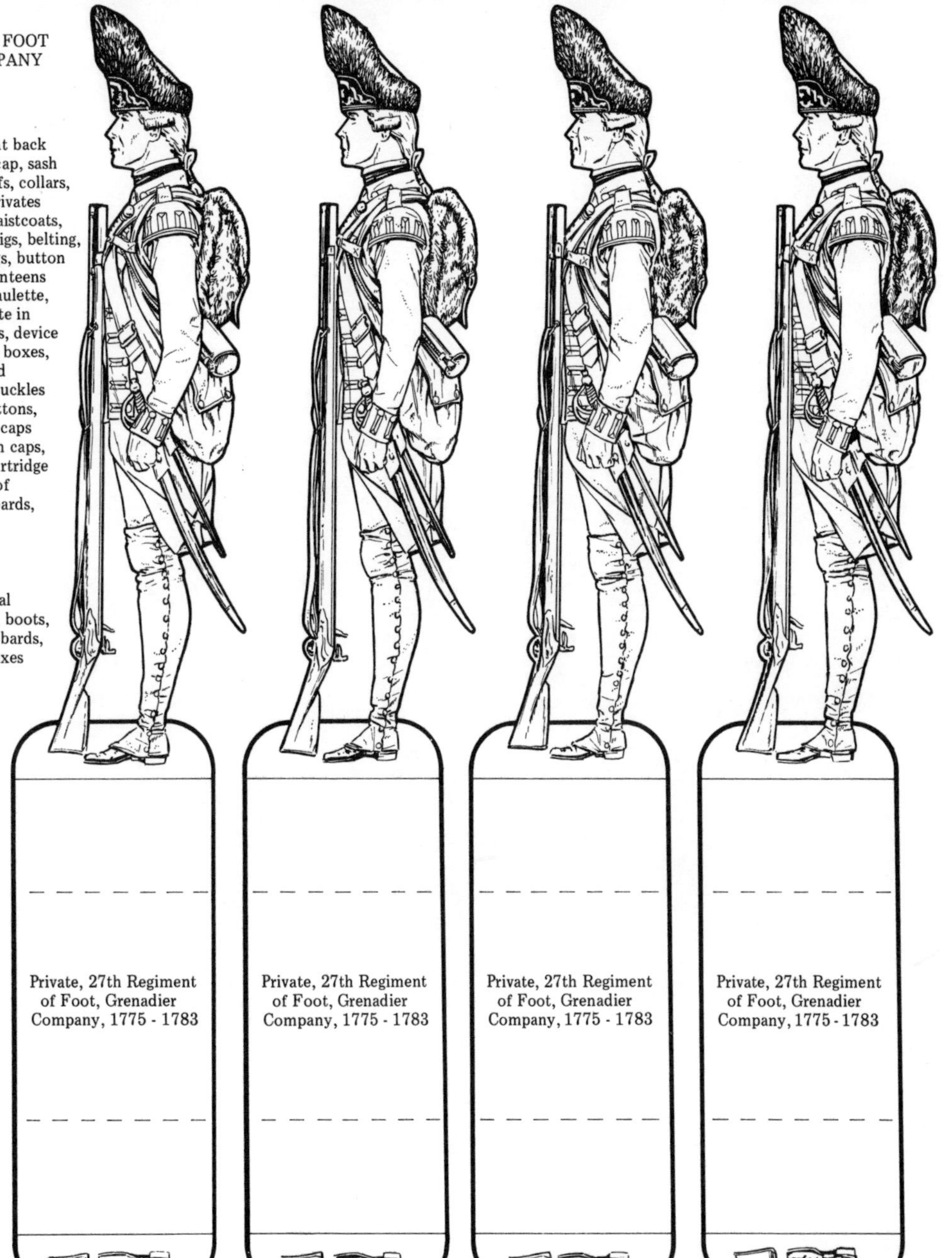

Company Officer
27th Regiment of Foot
Grenadier Company
1775 - 1783

Private, 27th Regiment
of Foot, Grenadier
Company, 1775 - 1783

Private, 27th Regiment
of Foot, Grenadier
Company, 1775 - 1783

Private, 27th Regiment
of Foot, Grenadier
Company, 1775 - 1783

Private, 27th Regiment
of Foot, Grenadier
Company, 1775 - 1783

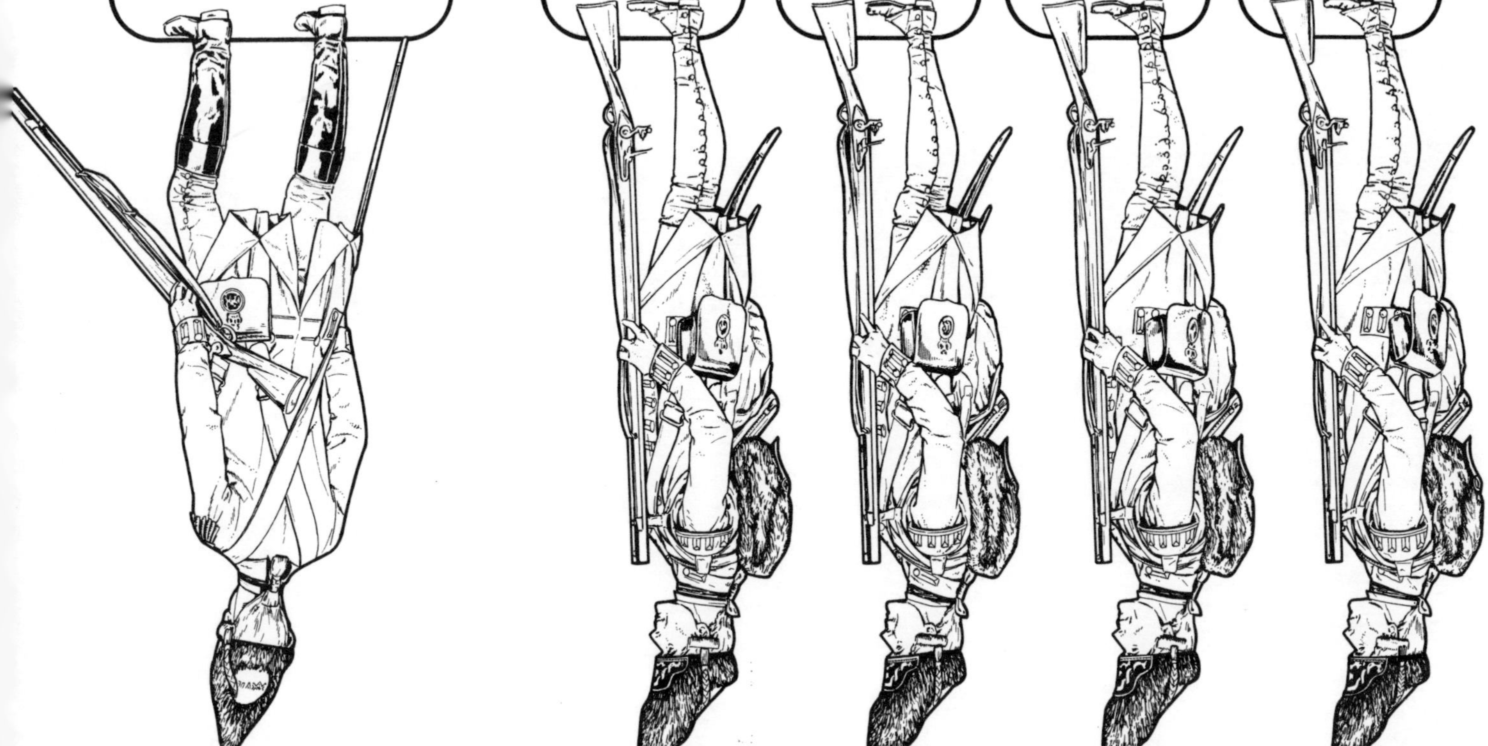

ROYAL ARTILLERY REGIMENT
1775 - 1783

Blue	Coats
Red	Coat facings, cuffs, collars, sergeant's sash
Yellow	Button hole lace, hat trim
Brass	Buttons, device on cartridge boxes, hilts and end caps on swords, butt plates, fore caps on muskets, telescope
White	Breeches, waist coats, stockings, musket slings, shoulder belts
Tan	Powder horns, rope
Black	Shoes, gaiters, hats, bayonet and sword scabbards, cartridge boxes

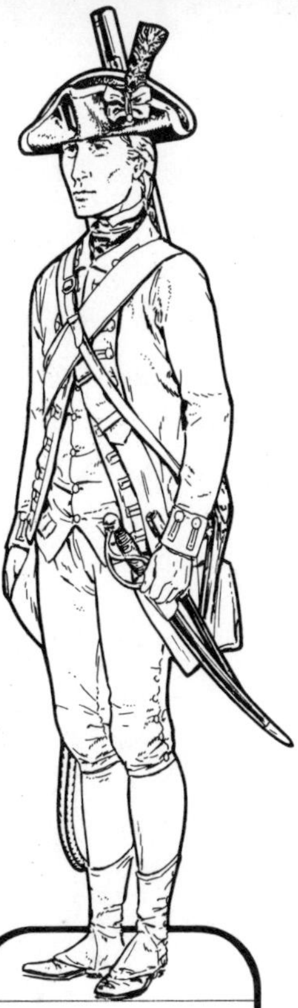

Private
Royal Artillery Regt.
1775 - 1783

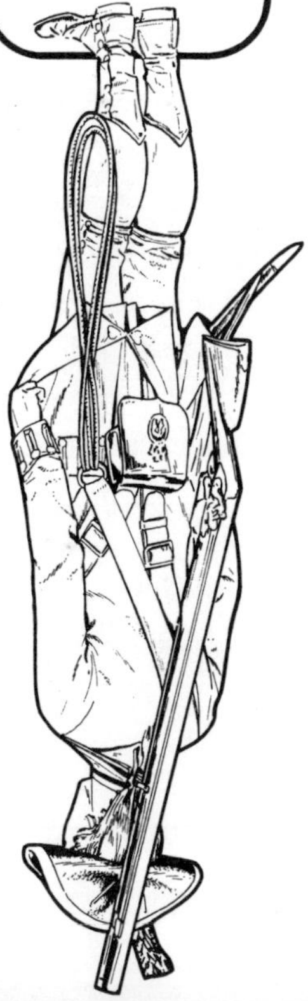

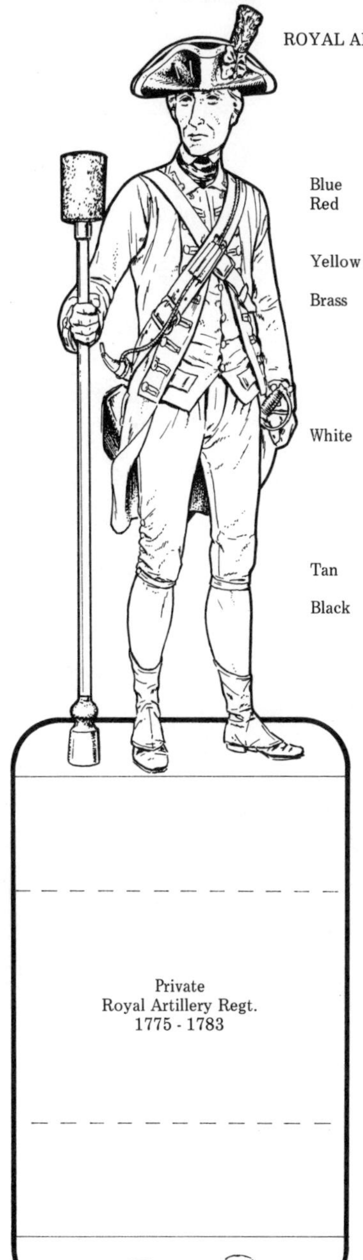

Private
Royal Artillery Regt.
1775 - 1783

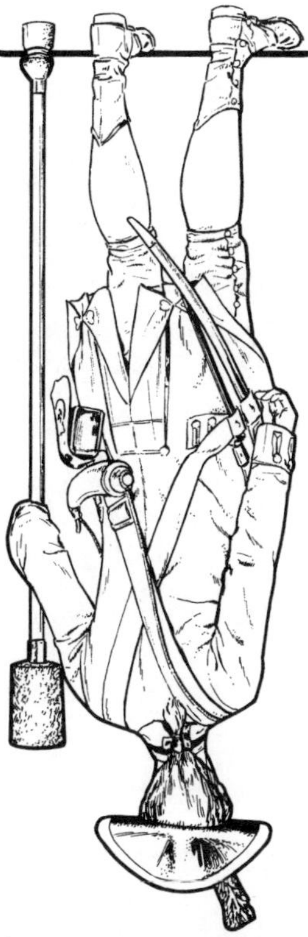

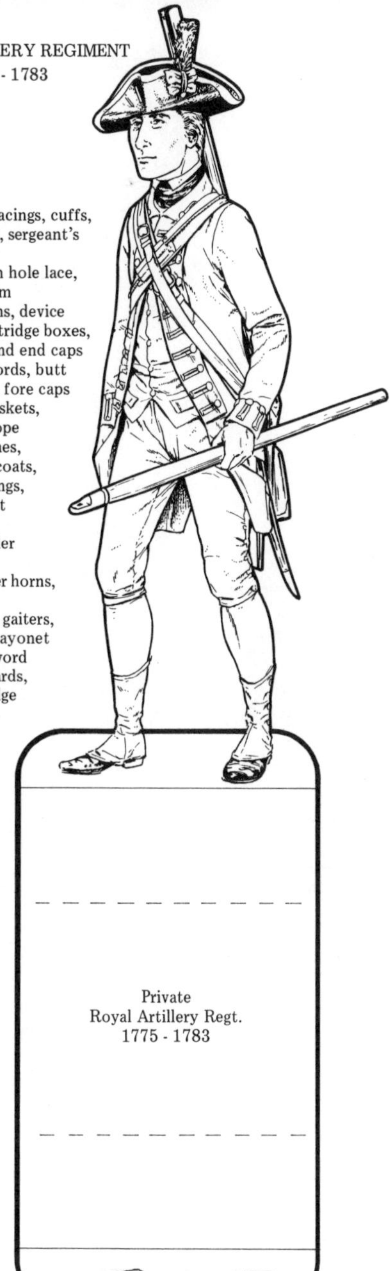

Private
Royal Artillery Regt.
1775 - 1783

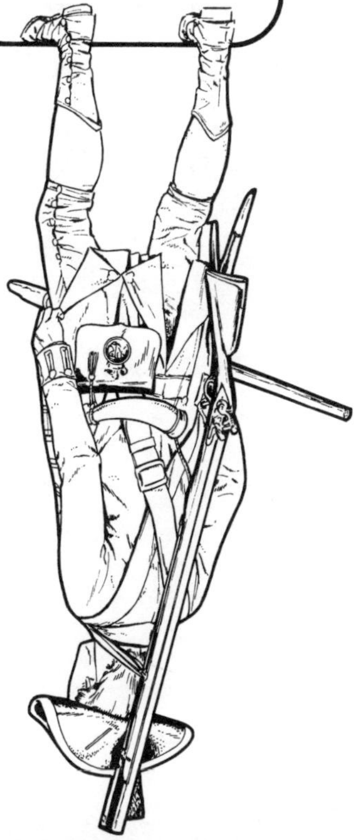

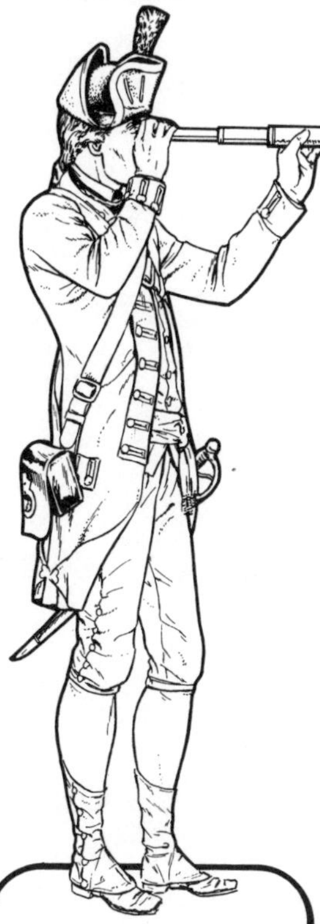

Sergeant
Royal Artillery Regt.
1775 - 1783

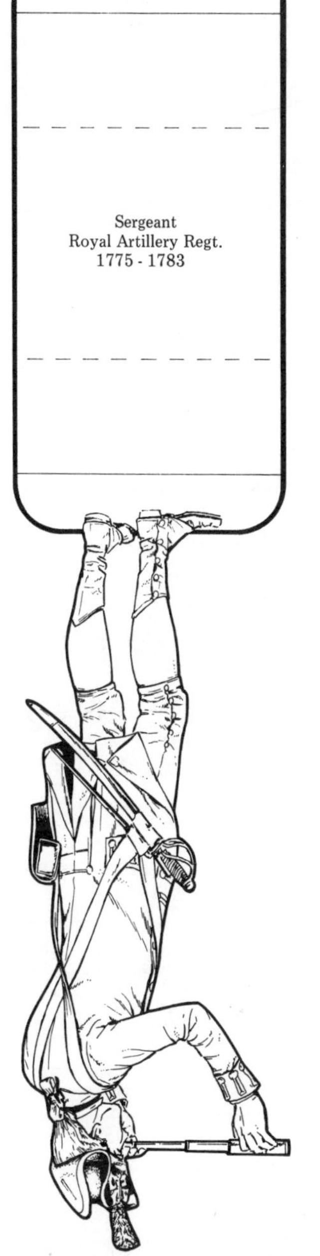

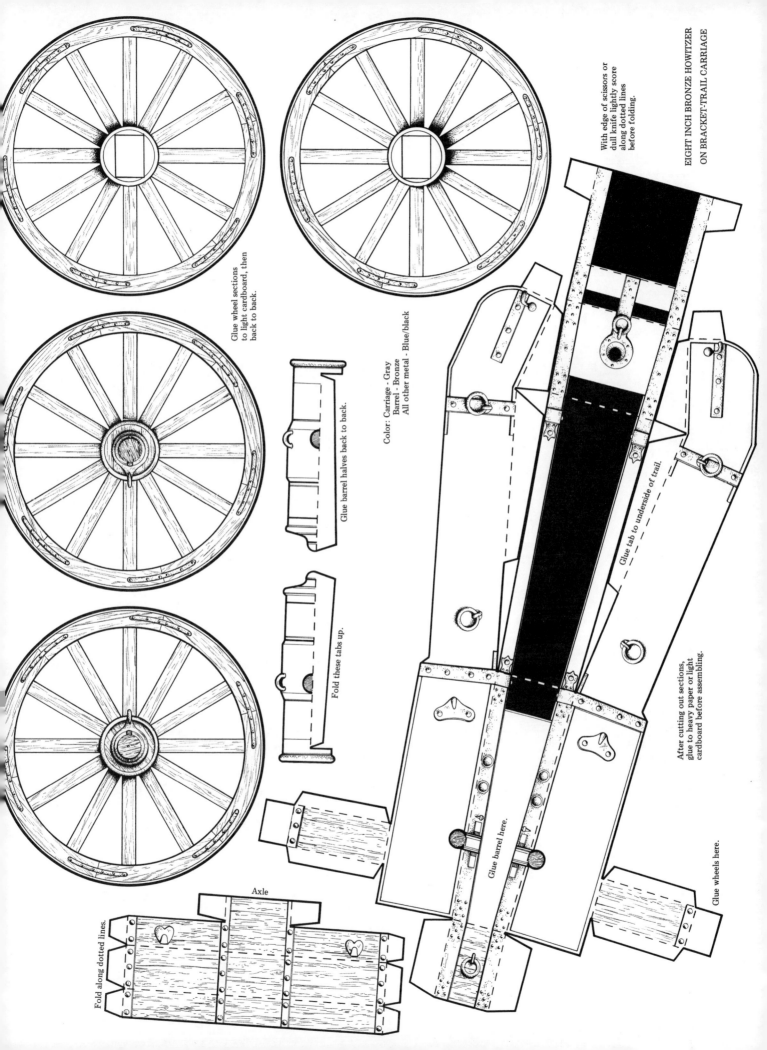

Glue wheel sections to light cardboard, then back to back.

Glue barrel halves back to back.

Fold these tabs up.

Color: Carriage - Gray
Barrel - Bronze
All other metal - Blue/black

With edge of scissors or dull knife lightly score along dotted lines before folding.

EIGHT INCH BRONZE HOWITZER ON BRACKET-TRAIL CARRIAGE

Glue tab to underside of trail.

After cutting out sections, glue to heavy paper or light cardboard before assembling.

Glue wheels here.

Glue barrel here.

Axle

Fold along dotted lines.

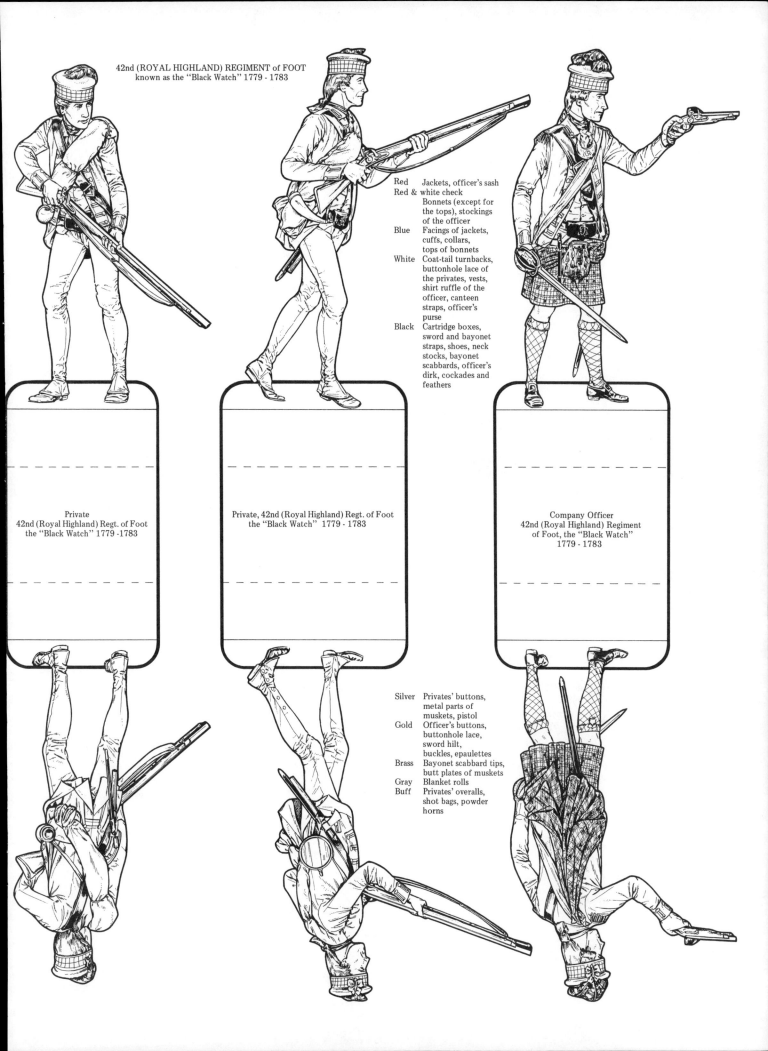

42nd (ROYAL HIGHLAND) REGIMENT of FOOT
known as the "Black Watch" 1779 - 1783

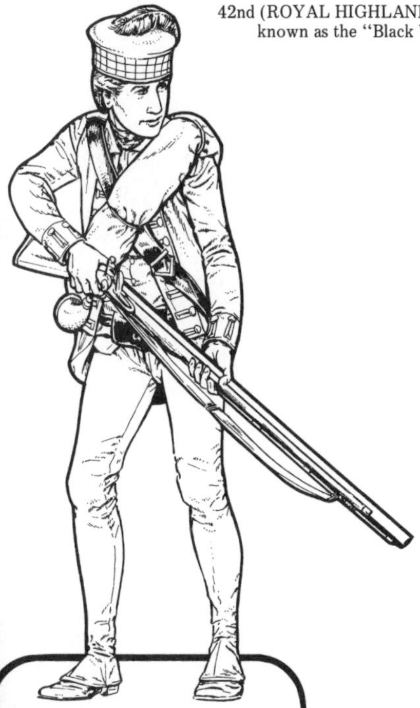

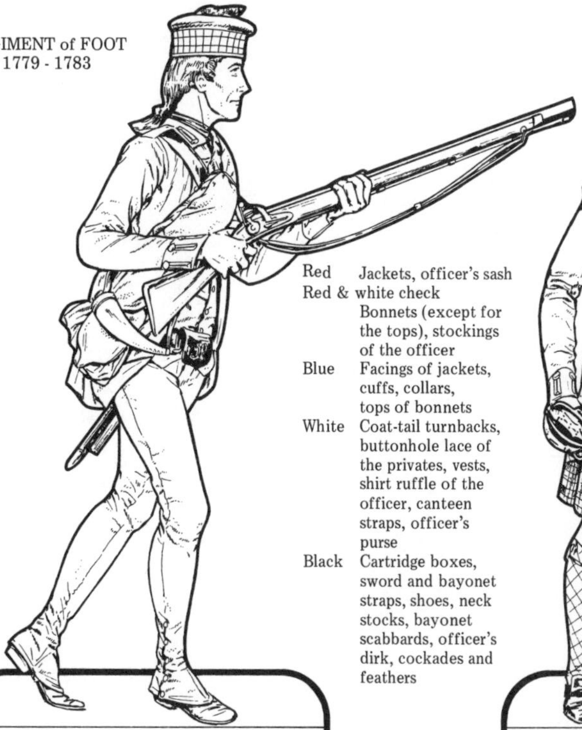

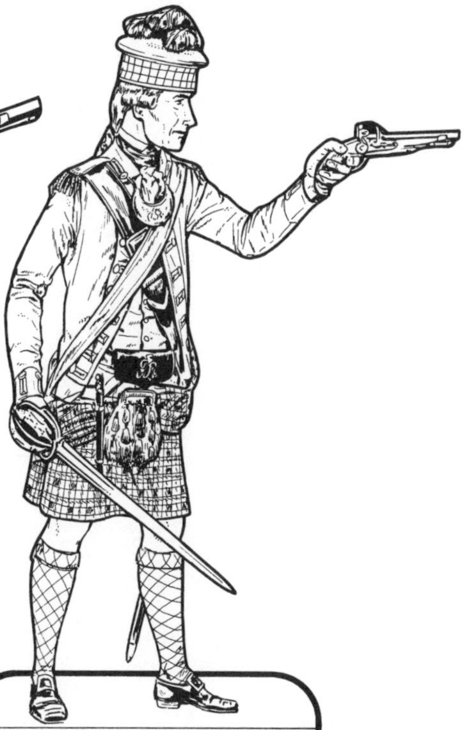

Red	Jackets, officer's sash
Red & white check	Bonnets (except for the tops), stockings of the officer
Blue	Facings of jackets, cuffs, collars, tops of bonnets
White	Coat-tail turnbacks, buttonhole lace of the privates, vests, shirt ruffle of the officer, canteen straps, officer's purse
Black	Cartridge boxes, sword and bayonet straps, shoes, neck stocks, bayonet scabbards, officer's dirk, cockades and feathers

Private
42nd (Royal Highland) Regt. of Foot
the "Black Watch" 1779 -1783

Private, 42nd (Royal Highland) Regt. of Foot
the "Black Watch" 1779 - 1783

Company Officer
42nd (Royal Highland) Regiment
of Foot, the "Black Watch"
1779 - 1783

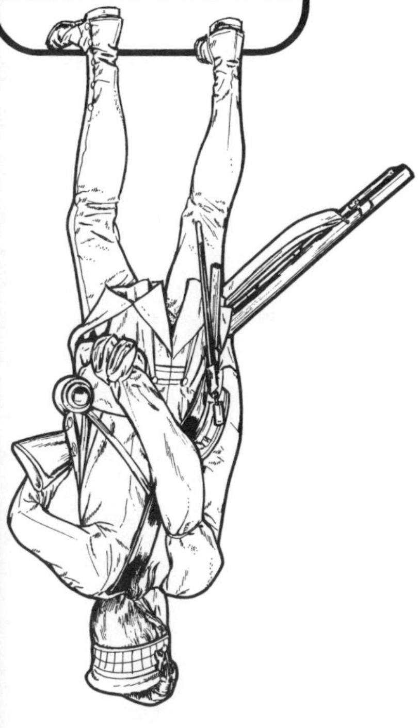

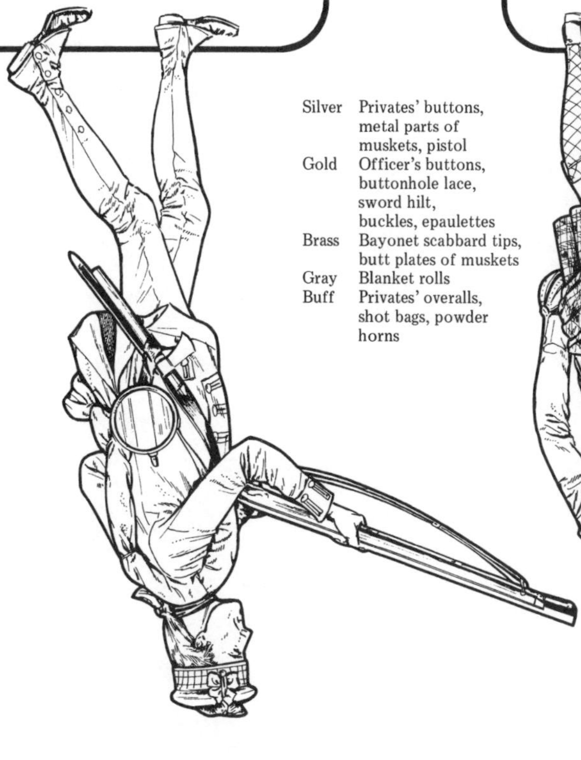

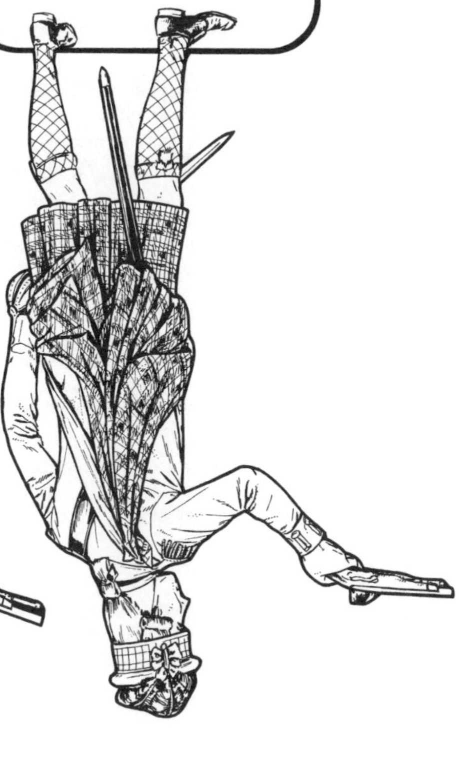

Silver	Privates' buttons, metal parts of muskets, pistol
Gold	Officer's buttons, buttonhole lace, sword hilt, buckles, epaulettes
Brass	Bayonet scabbard tips, butt plates of muskets
Gray	Blanket rolls
Buff	Privates' overalls, shot bags, powder horns

84th REGIMENT of FOOT (*ROYAL HIGHLAND EMIGRANTS*)
1775 - 1783

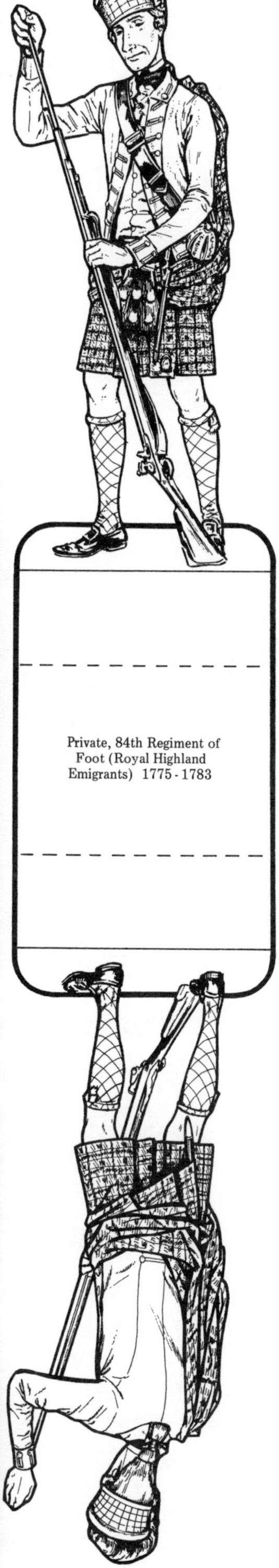
Private, 84th Regiment of Foot (Royal Highland Emigrants) 1775 - 1783

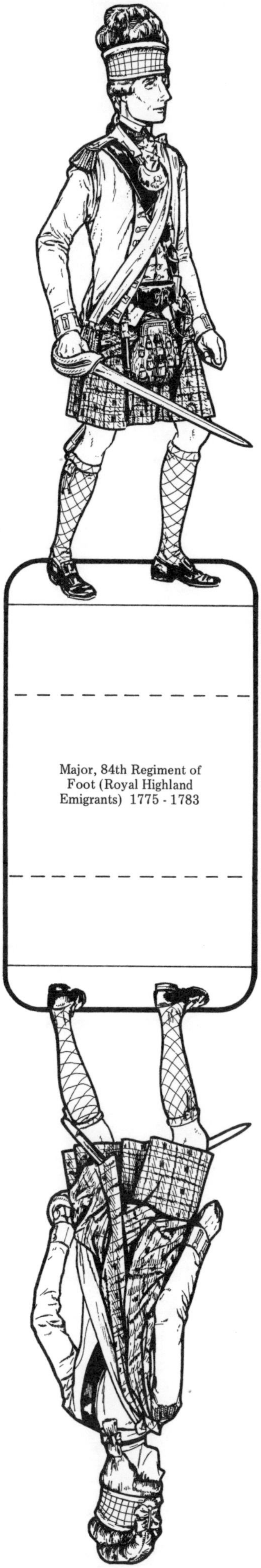
Major, 84th Regiment of Foot (Royal Highland Emigrants) 1775 - 1783

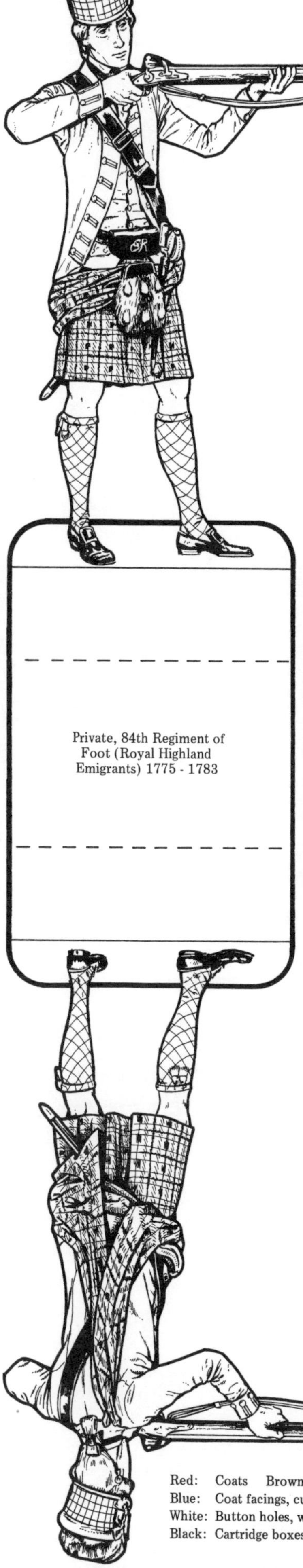
Private, 84th Regiment of Foot (Royal Highland Emigrants) 1775 - 1783

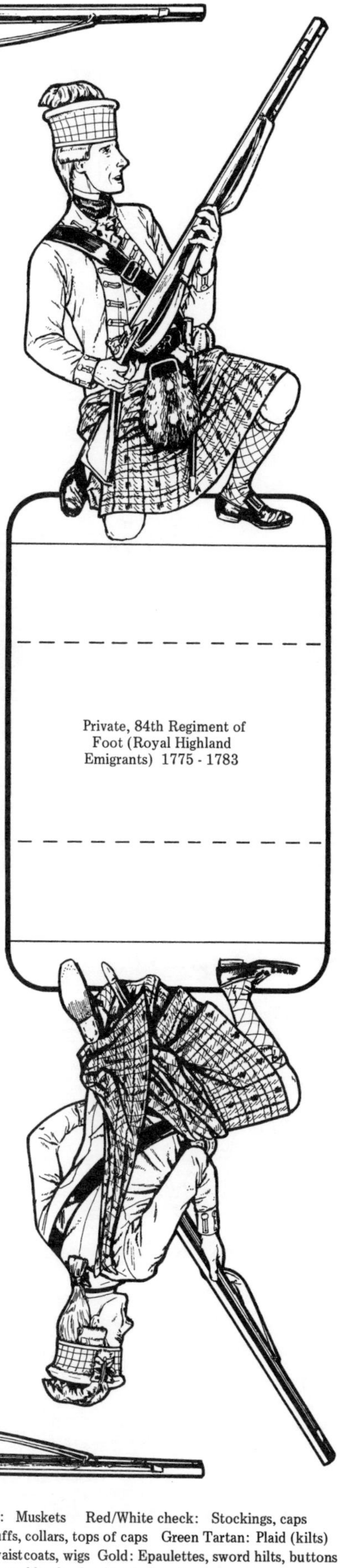
Private, 84th Regiment of Foot (Royal Highland Emigrants) 1775 - 1783

Red: Coats Brown: Muskets Red/White check: Stockings, caps
Blue: Coat facings, cuffs, collars, tops of caps Green Tartan: Plaid (kilts)
White: Button holes, waistcoats, wigs Gold: Epaulettes, sword hilts, buttons
Black: Cartridge boxes, scabbards, shoulder belts, plumes

QUEEN'S RANGERS, 1776 - 1783
Sergeant of Hussar troop

Green	Jacket, breeches, "bag" of hat, saddle cloth
Blue	Cuffs, collar
Silver	Lace around cuffs, collar, epaulettes, crescent device on hat, buttons, stirrups
White	Crescents on saddle cloth, tassel on hat
Black	Sword belt, scabbard, boots, pistol cases
Brown	Hat, saddle bags, saddle, harness
Gray	Blanket roll

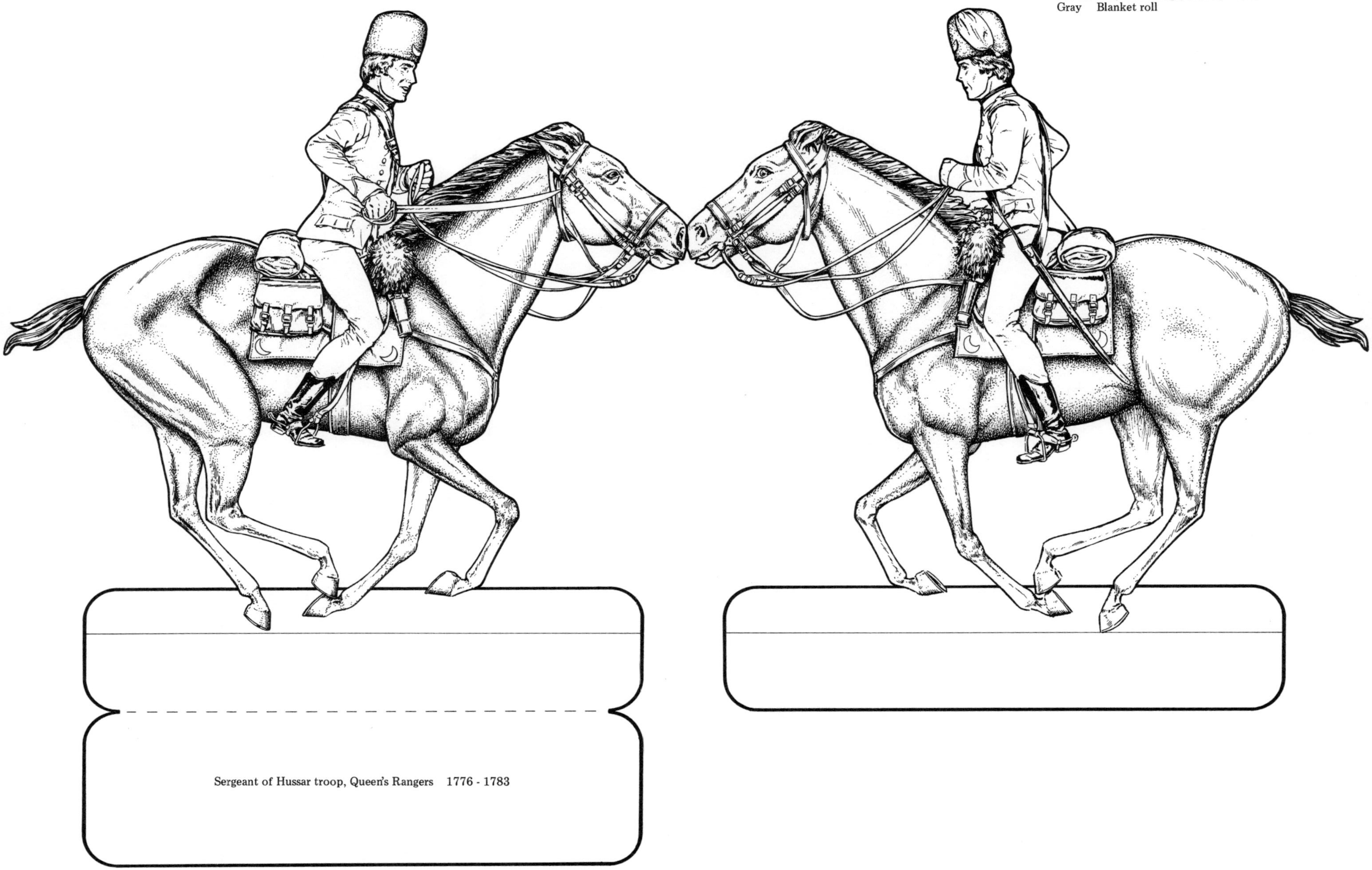
Sergeant of Hussar troop, Queen's Rangers 1776 - 1783

PRINCE OF WALES' AMERICAN REGIMENT
1777 - 1783

Red	Coats, sash of sergeant
Green	Facings, cuffs
Yellow	Buttons, sword hilt, belt plates, cipher device on cartridge boxes
White	Button holes, binding of hats, cross belts, waist coats, breeches, gun sling, turnbacks
Black	Hats, cartridge boxes, sword scabbards, bayonet scabbards, shoes
Brown	Muskets, halberd shaft

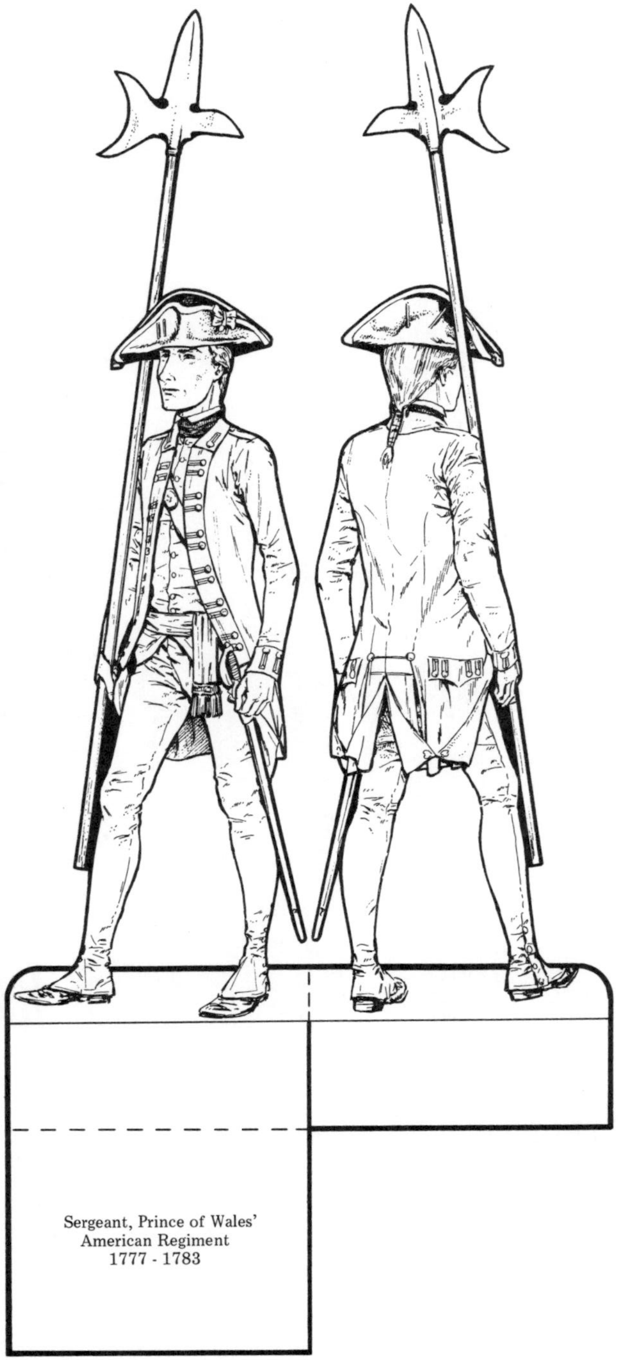
Sergeant, Prince of Wales'
American Regiment
1777 - 1783

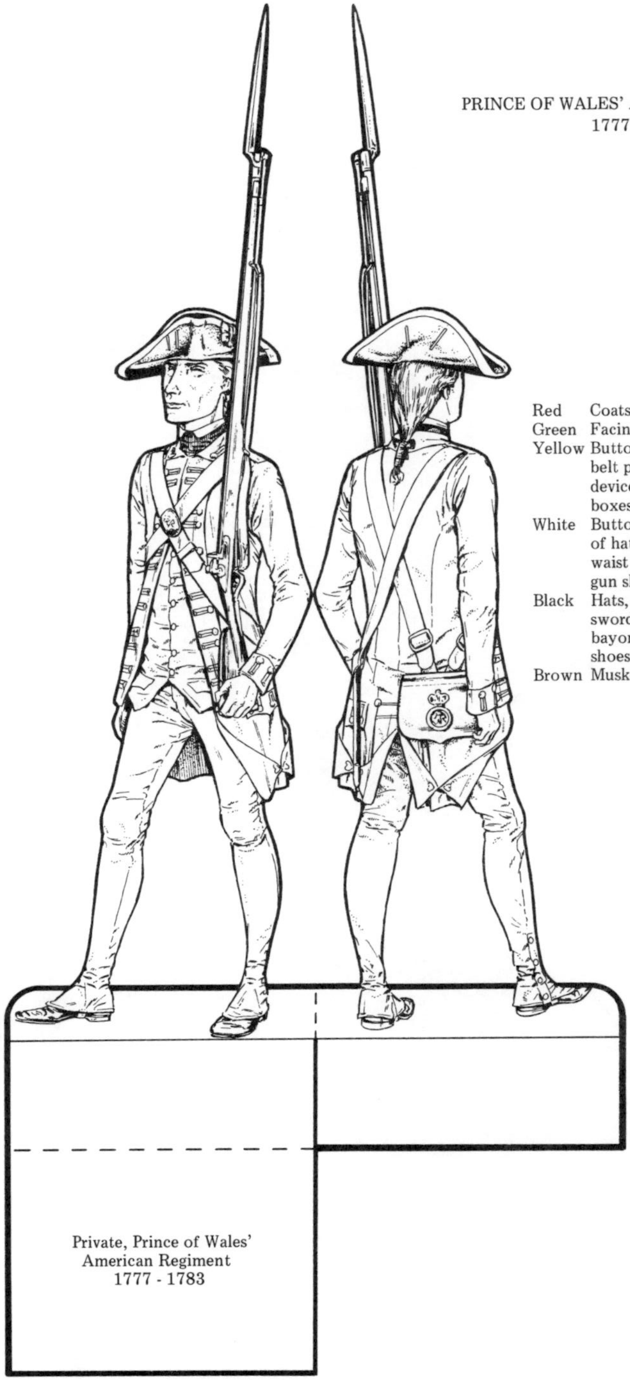
Private, Prince of Wales'
American Regiment
1777 - 1783

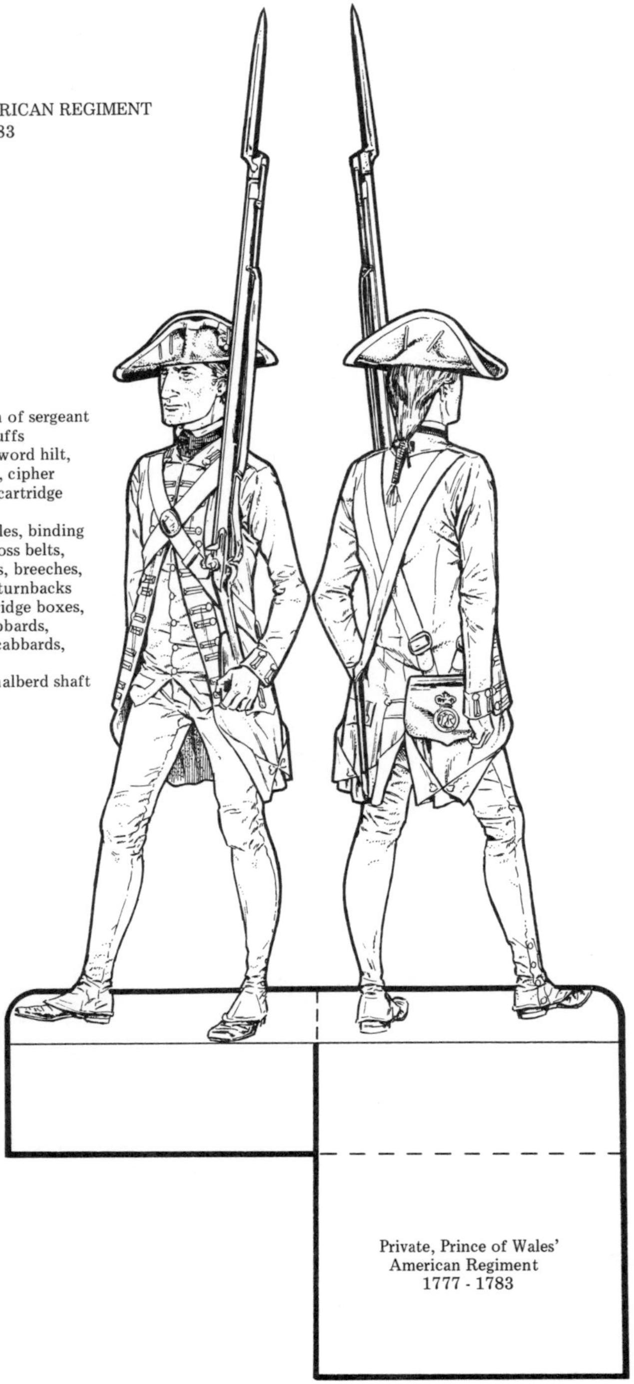
Private, Prince of Wales'
American Regiment
1777 - 1783

CHIEF JOSEPH BRANT & BUTLER'S RANGERS, 1777

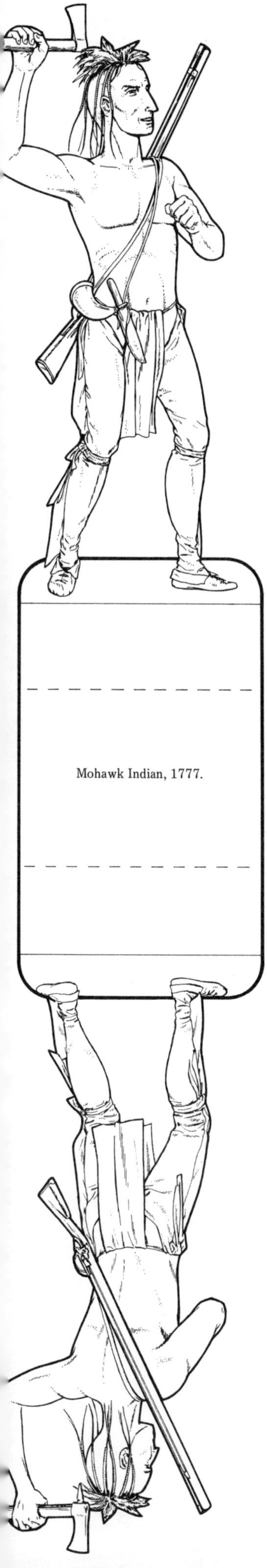
Mohawk Indian, 1777.

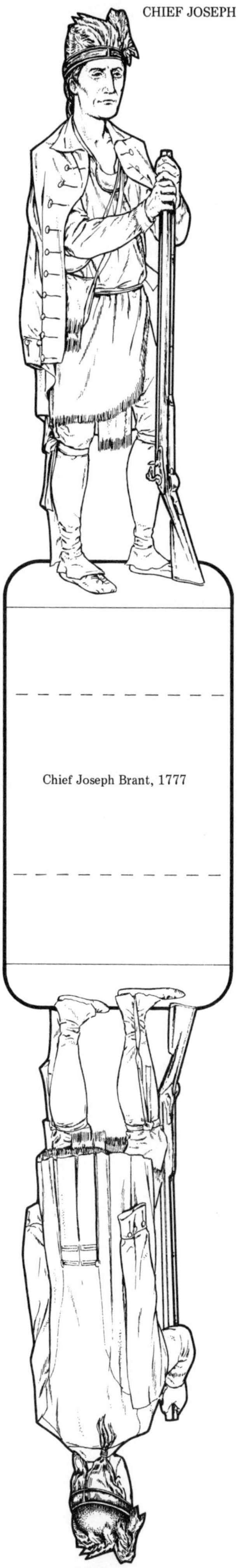
Chief Joseph Brant, 1777

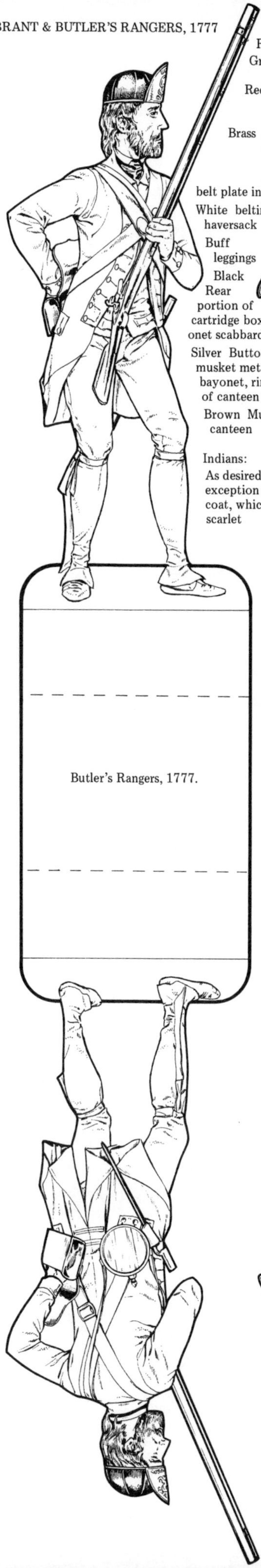
Butler's Rangers, 1777.

Rangers:
Green Coats, waistcoats
Red Coat facings, cuffs, collars, linings
Brass Front plate of cap, butt plate, forecap of muskets, belt plate in front
White belting haversack
Buff leggings
Black Rear portion of caps, cartridge boxes, bayonet scabbard
Silver Buttons, musket metal, bayonet, rim of canteen
Brown Muskets, canteen

Indians:
As desired, with the exception of the Chief's coat, which should be scarlet

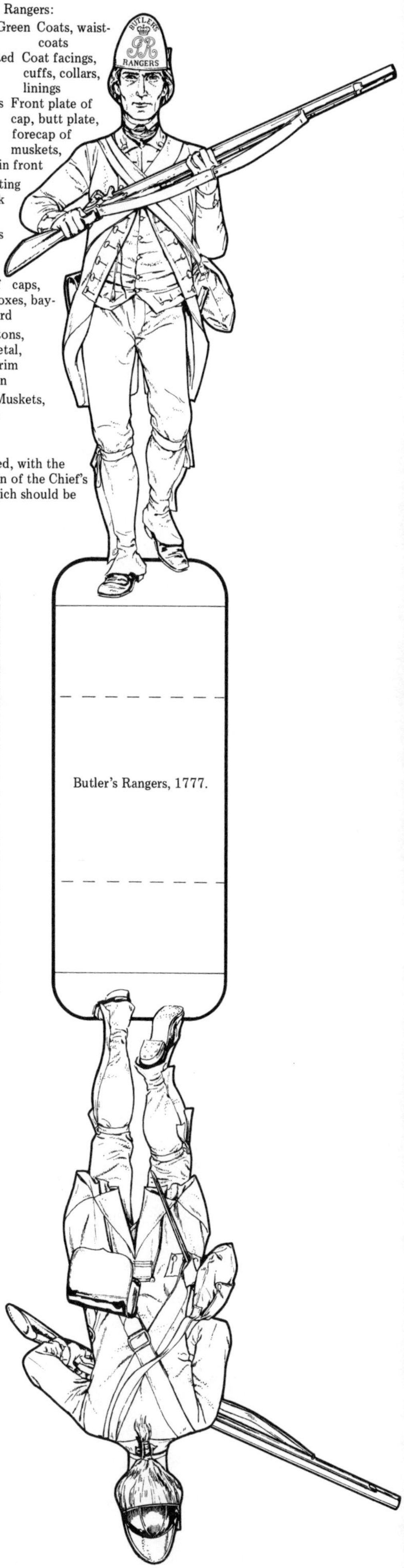
BUTLER'S
GR
RANGERS
Butler's Rangers, 1777.

JOHNSON'S ROYAL GREENS
KING'S ROYAL REGIMENT
of NEW YORK 1776 - 1783

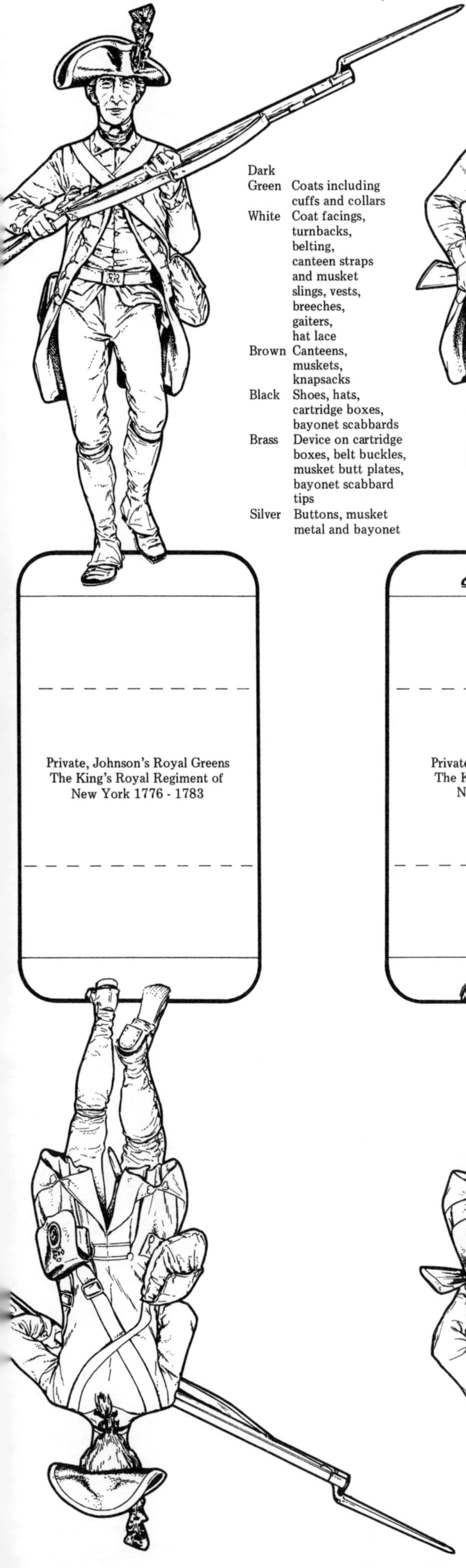
Private, Johnson's Royal Greens
The King's Royal Regiment of
New York 1776 - 1783

Dark Green	Coats including cuffs and collars
White	Coat facings, turnbacks, belting, canteen straps and musket slings, vests, breeches, gaiters, hat lace
Brown	Canteens, muskets, knapsacks
Black	Shoes, hats, cartridge boxes, bayonet scabbards
Brass	Device on cartridge boxes, belt buckles, musket butt plates, bayonet scabbard tips
Silver	Buttons, musket metal and bayonet

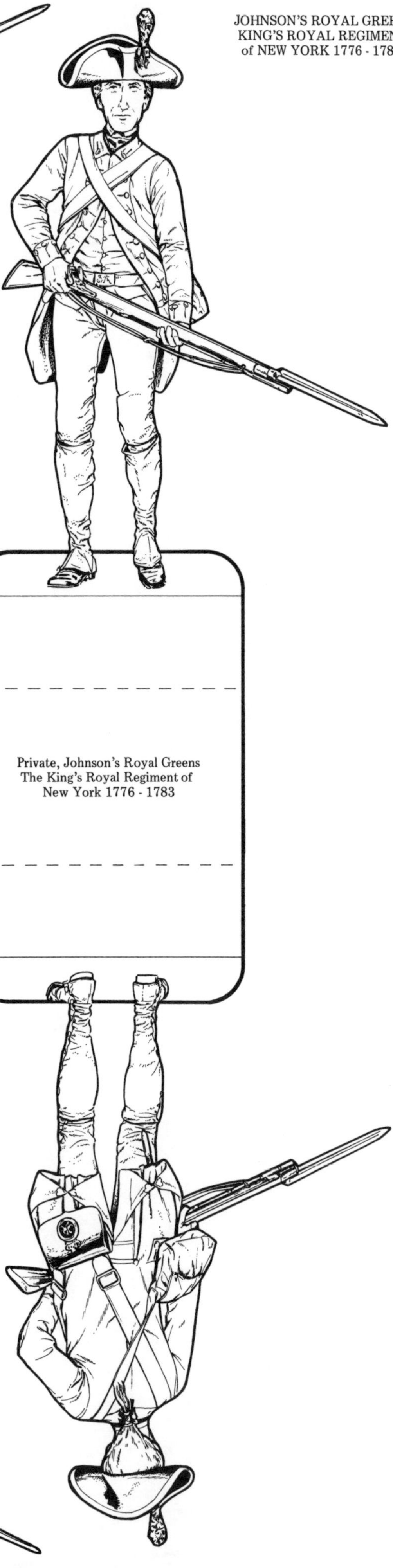
Private, Johnson's Royal Greens
The King's Royal Regiment of
New York 1776 - 1783

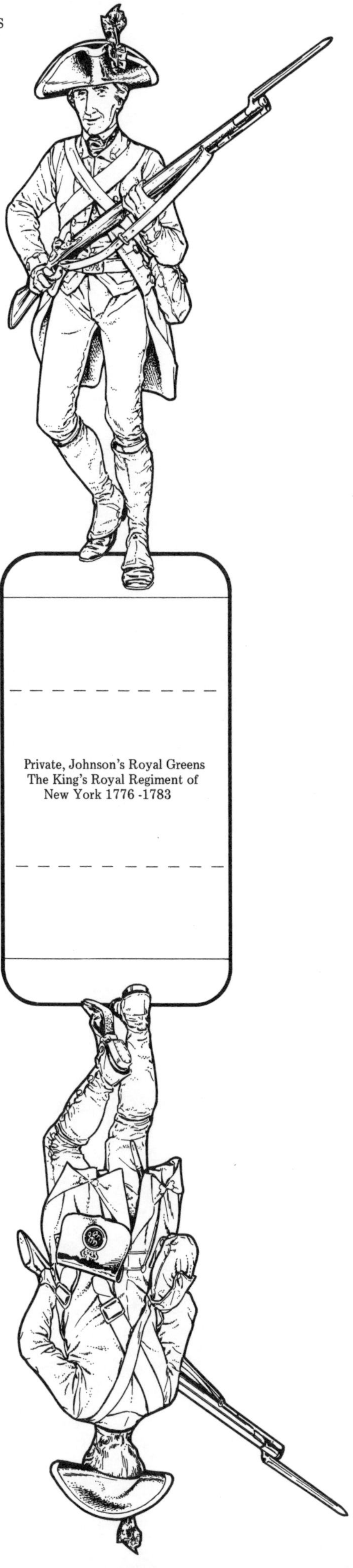
Private, Johnson's Royal Greens
The King's Royal Regiment of
New York 1776 -1783

HESSE-CASSEL FELD JAEGER KORPS zu PFERD
(Light Horse or "Chasseurs") 1776 - 1783

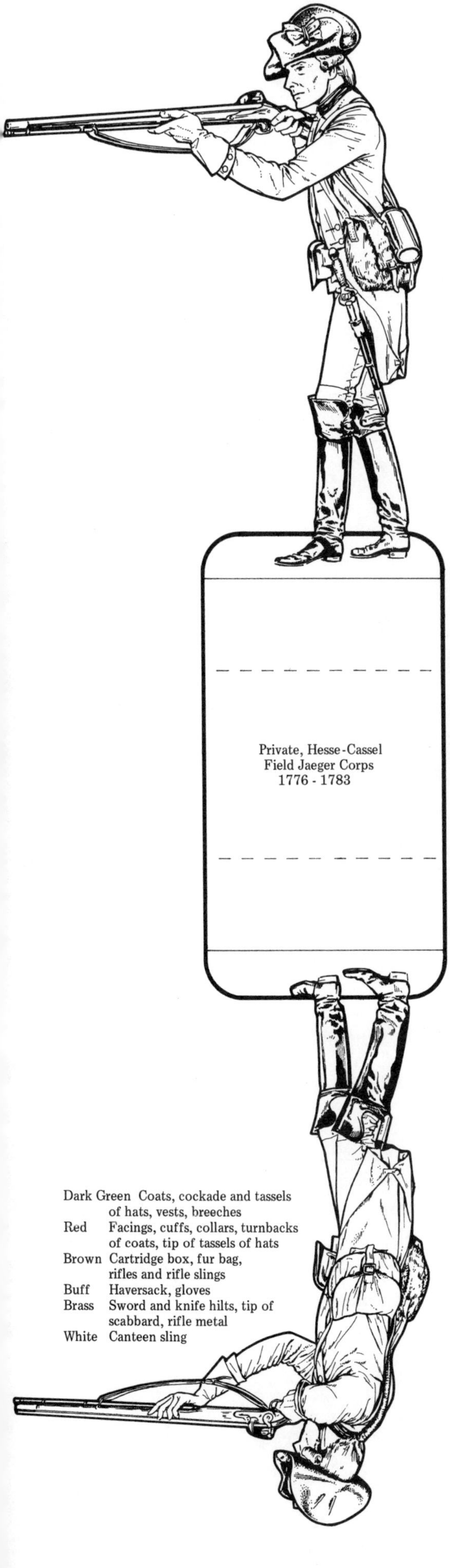
Private, Hesse-Cassel
Field Jaeger Corps
1776 - 1783

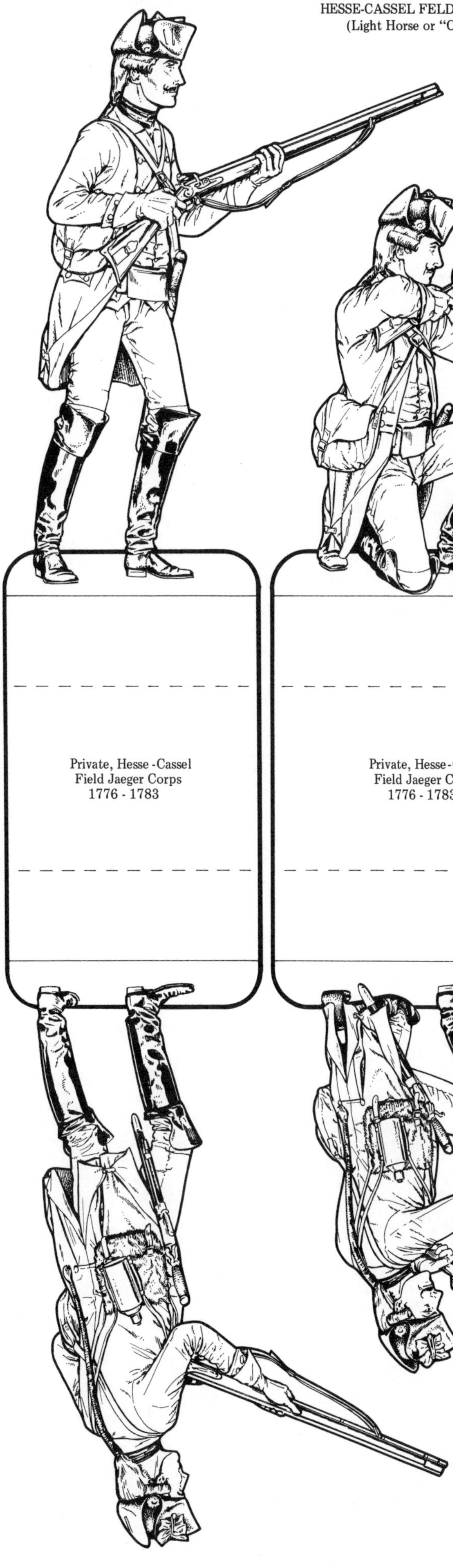
Private, Hesse-Cassel
Field Jaeger Corps
1776 - 1783

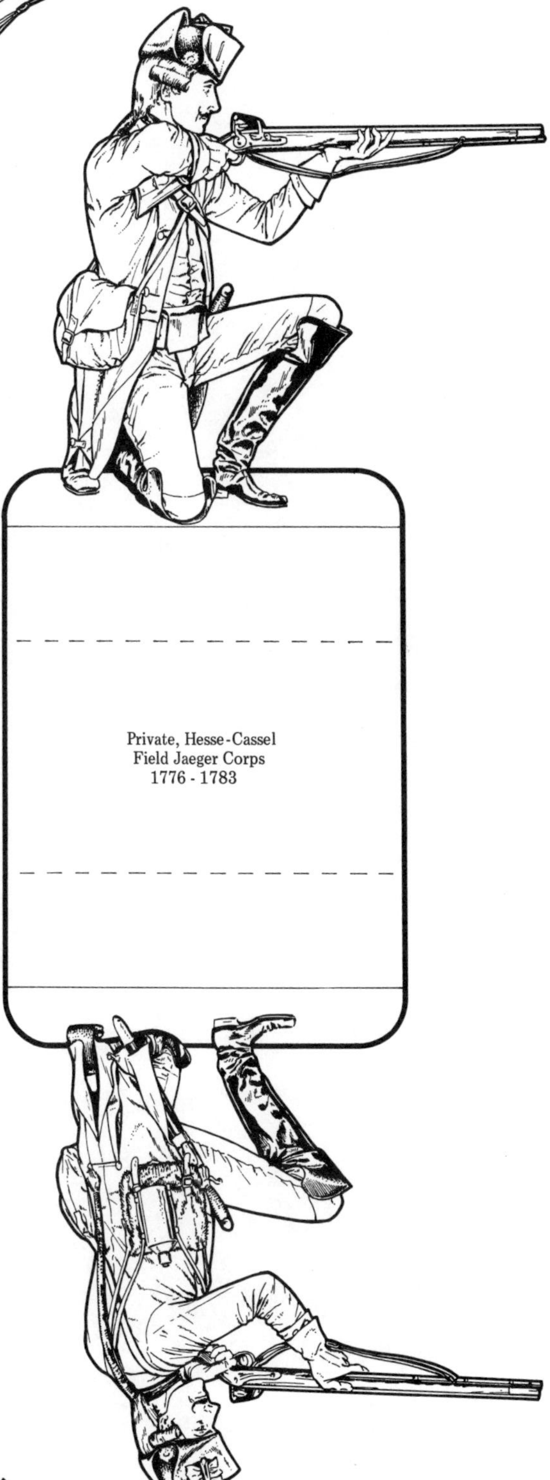
Private, Hesse-Cassel
Field Jaeger Corps
1776 - 1783

Dark Green Coats, cockade and tassels of hats, vests, breeches
Red Facings, cuffs, collars, turnbacks of coats, tip of tassels of hats
Brown Cartridge box, fur bag, rifles and rifle slings
Buff Haversack, gloves
Brass Sword and knife hilts, tip of scabbard, rifle metal
White Canteen sling

GRENADIER REGIMENT VON RALL
1776 - 1783

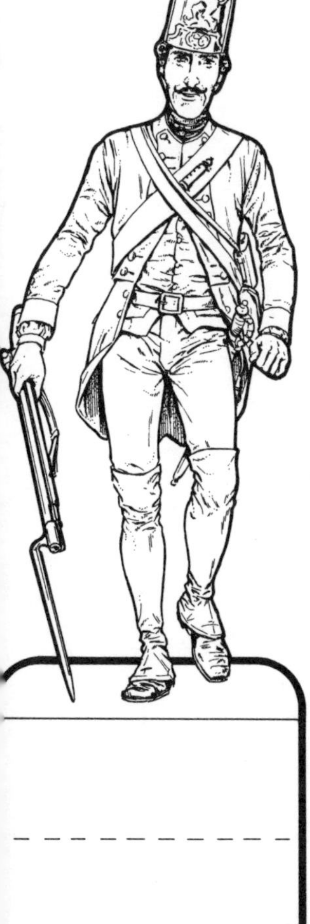

Private, Grenadier Regt. von Rall
1776 - 1783

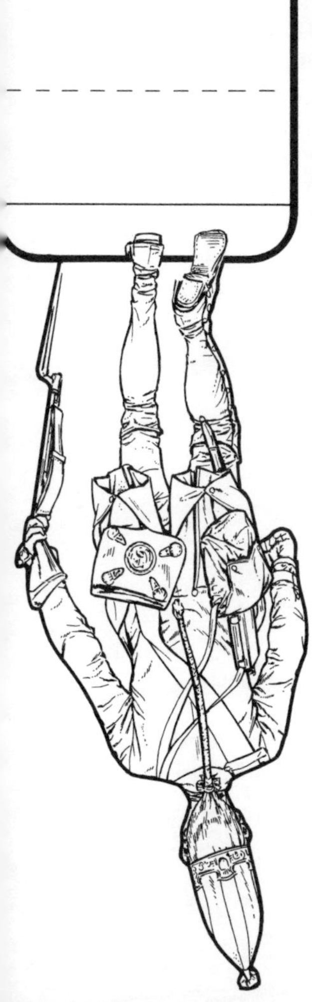

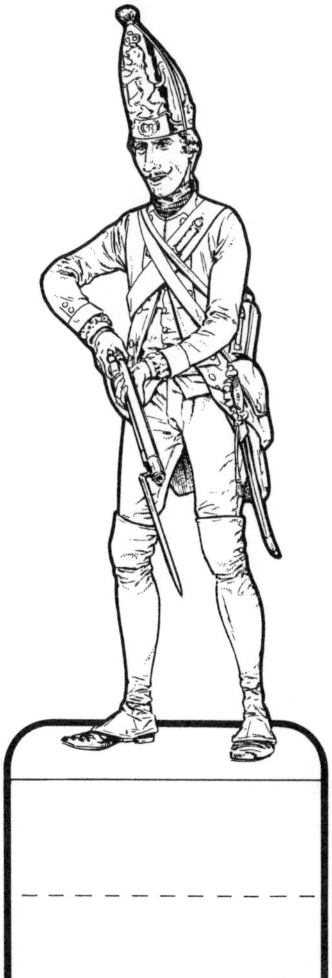

Private, Grenadier Regiment von Rall
1776 - 1783

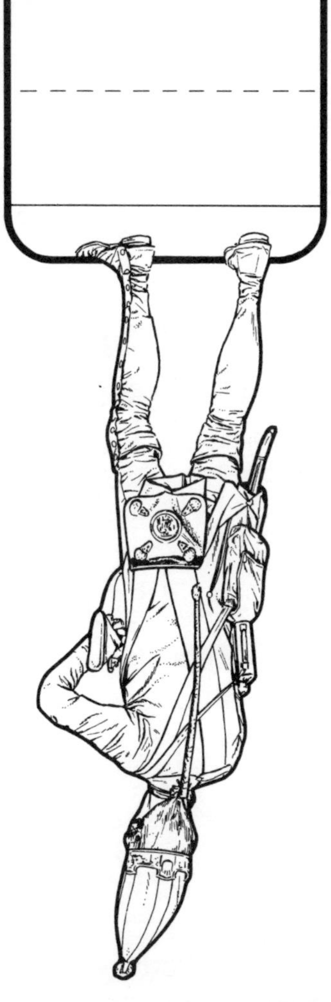

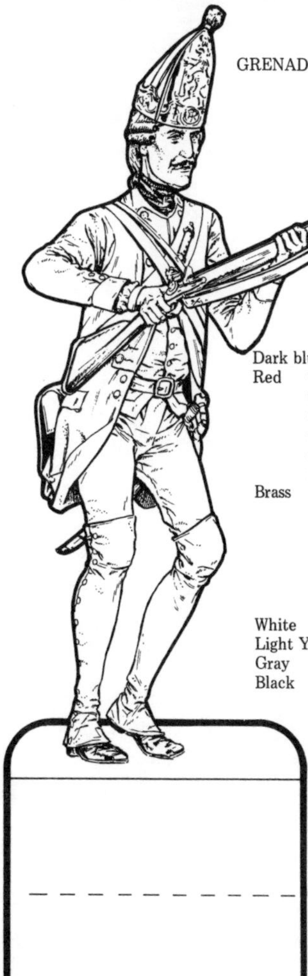

Dark blue Coats
Red Collars, cuffs, lapels, turnbacks, backs of caps (with white tapes), pompons on caps, shoulder straps, musket slings
Brass Cap plates (fronts) and bases, buttons, devices on cartridge boxes, match holders on shoulder straps, butt caps of muskets, sword hilts and end caps
White Belting, canteen, hair
Light Yellow Vests, breeches
Gray Haversacks
Black Musket stocks, shoes, neck cloths, cartridge boxes, gaiters, sword scabbards

Private, Grenadier Regt. von Rall
1776 - 1783

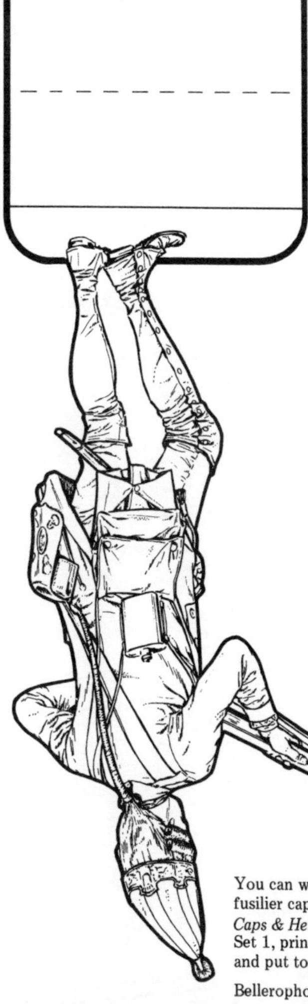

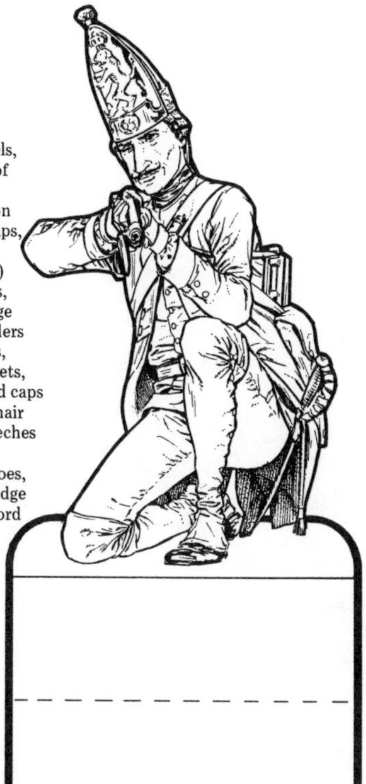

Private, Grenadier Regiment von Rall
1776 - 1783

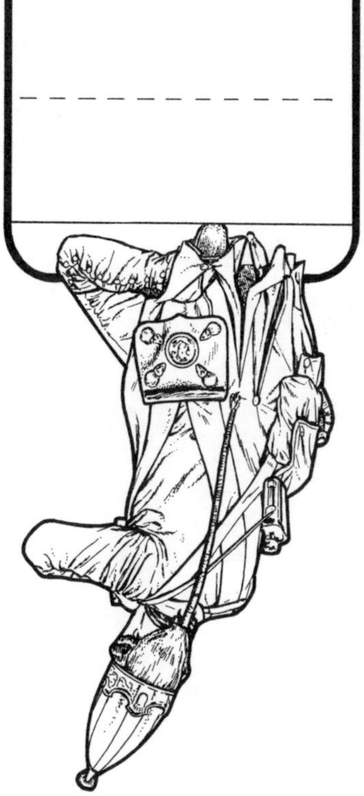

BRUNSWICK REGIMENT OF DRAGOONS
1776 - 1783

Light Blue Coats
Yellow Facings, linings, vests, buttons
White Aiguillettes, plumes on hats, gauntlets, belting, cartridge boxes
Buff Breeches
Black Boots, hats, sword scabbards
Brown Muskets

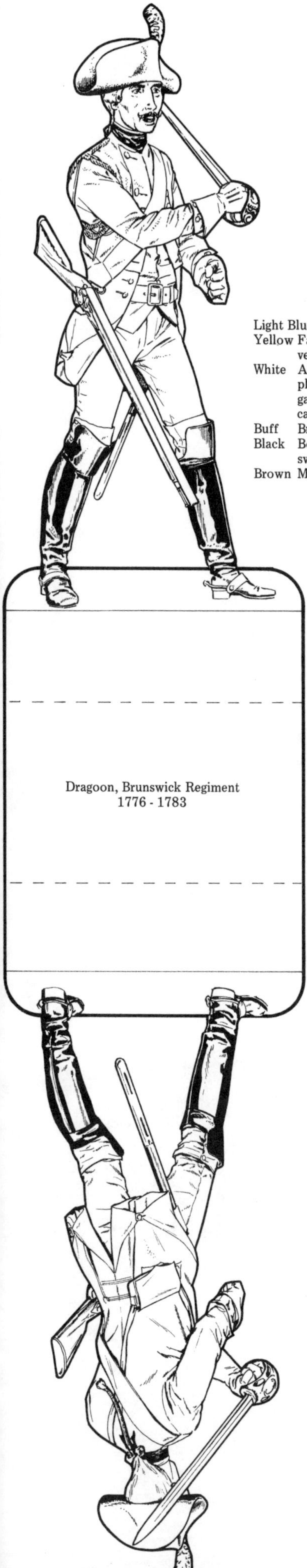

Dragoon, Brunswick Regiment
1776 - 1783

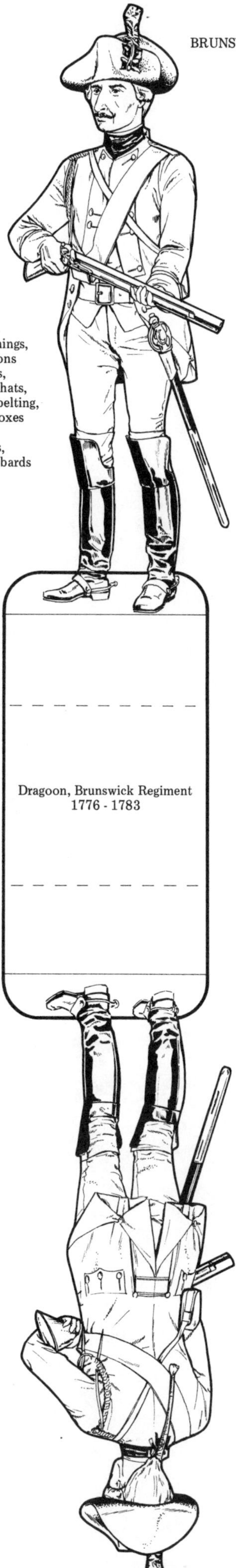

Dragoon, Brunswick Regiment
1776 - 1783

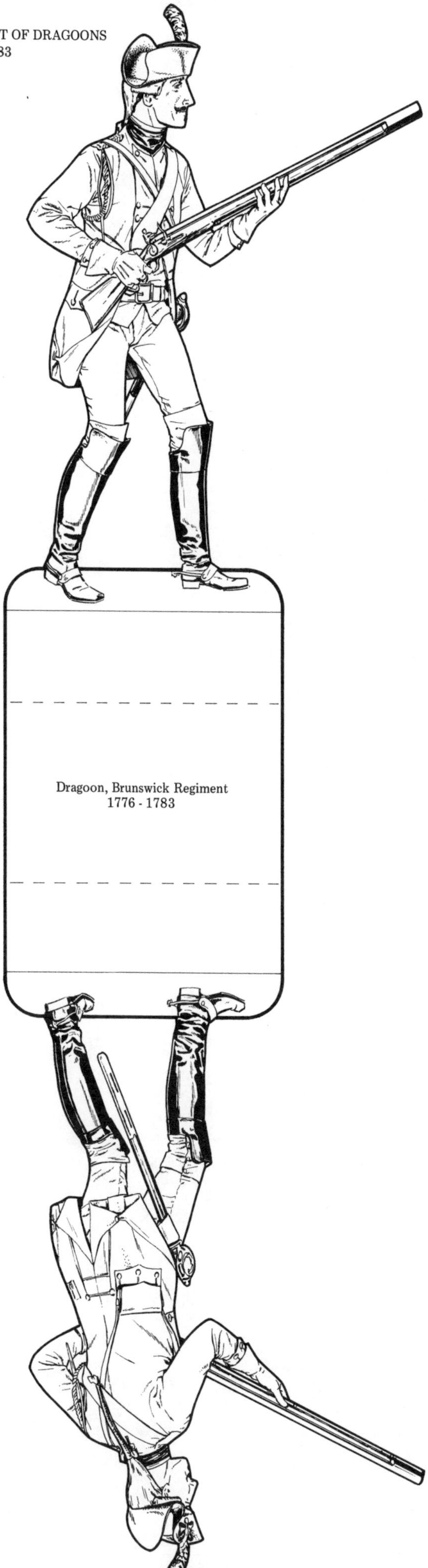

Dragoon, Brunswick Regiment
1776 - 1783

BRUNSWICK INFANTRY REGIMENT VON RHETZ, 1776 - 1777

Blue	Coats
White	Collars, lapels, cuffs, privates' breeches,

Blue	Coats
White	Collars, lapels, cuffs privates' breeches, vests, privates' hat lace, haversacks, straps of haversacks and cartridge boxes, musket slings
Red	Linings, turnbacks of coats, pompons of privates, sword knots of privates
Yellow	Buttons, sash of officer
Gold	Officer's hat lace, gorget, scabbard tips
Brown	Knapsack, scabbards, muskets
Black	Officer's breeches and boots, all hats, cartridge boxes, neck stocks, shoes

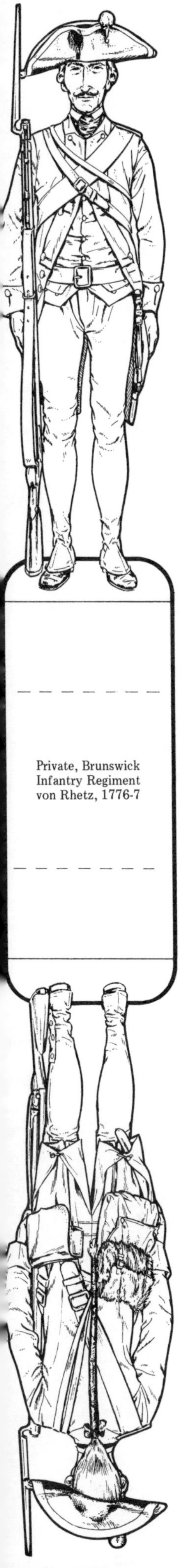
Private, Brunswick Infantry Regiment von Rhetz, 1776-7

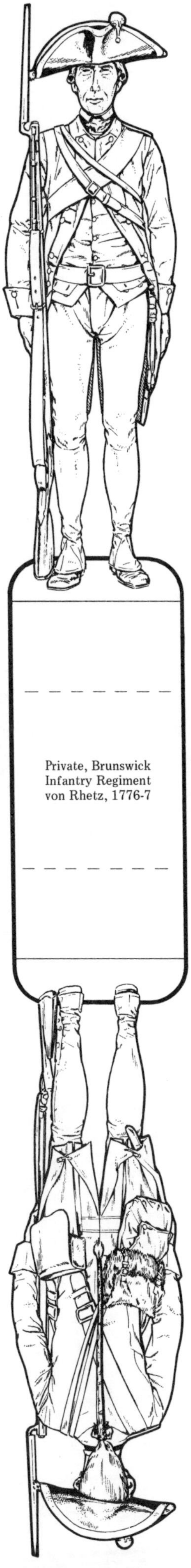
Private, Brunswick Infantry Regiment von Rhetz, 1776-7

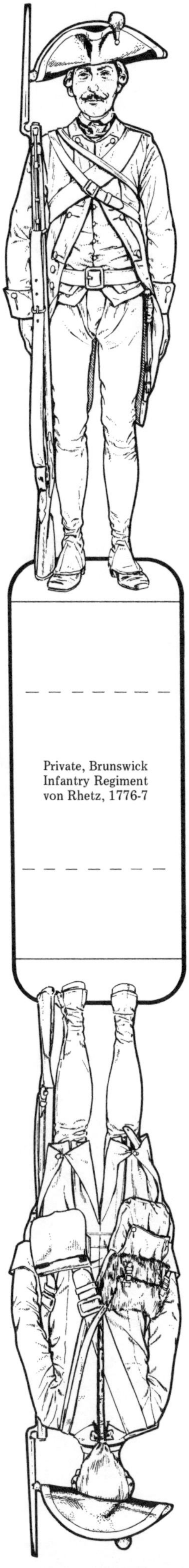
Private, Brunswick Infantry Regiment von Rhetz, 1776-7

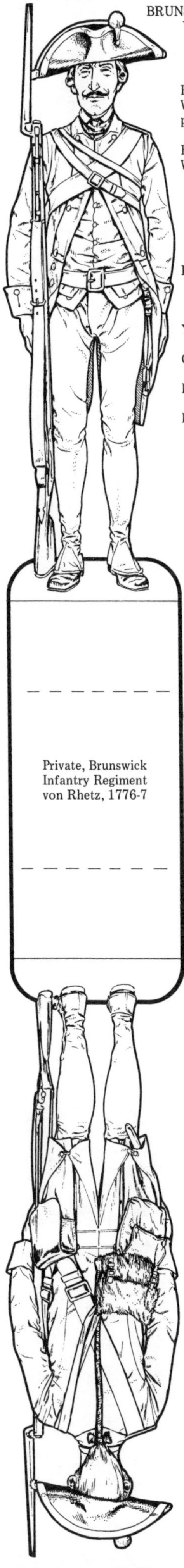
Private, Brunswick Infantry Regiment von Rhetz, 1776-7

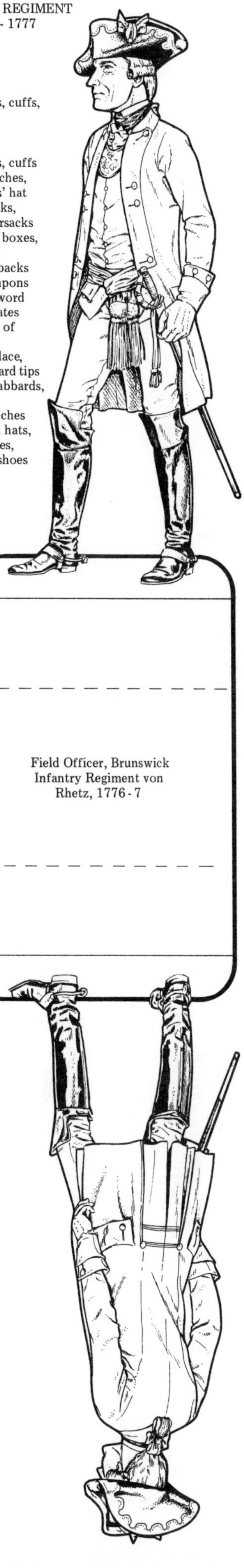
Field Officer, Brunswick Infantry Regiment von Rhetz, 1776 - 7